The Greatest Surfriders from Duke Kahanamoku to Kelly Slater

LEGENDS OF SURFING

DUKE BOYD

Photography by Jeff Divine

Foreword by Steve Pezman

MVP
BOOKS

First published in 2009 by MVP Books, an imprint of Quarto Publishing Group USA Inc.,
400 First Avenue North, Suite 400, Minneapolis, MN 55401 USA

Text © 2009 Duke Boyd

MVP Books are also available at discounts in bulk quantity for industrial or sales-
promotional use. For details write to Special Sales Manager at Quarto Publishing Group
USA Inc., 400 First Avenue North, Suite 400, Minneapolis, MN 55401 USA.

To find out more, visit us online at www.MVPBooks.com.

ISBN: 978-0-7603-4703-4

Editor: Michael Dregni
Design Manager: LeAnn Kuhlmann
Design by: Sarah Bennett
Printed in China

On the frontispiece: Walter Hoffman. *Walter Hoffman collection*
Opposite the title page: Kelly Slater.

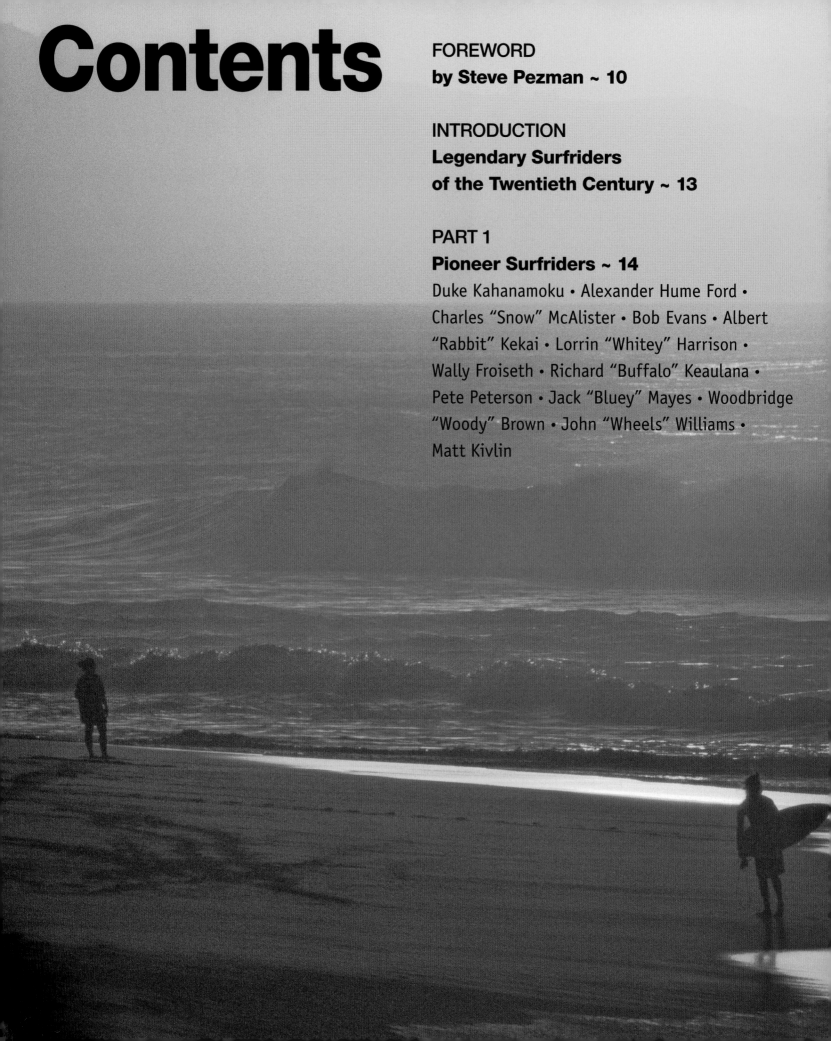

Contents

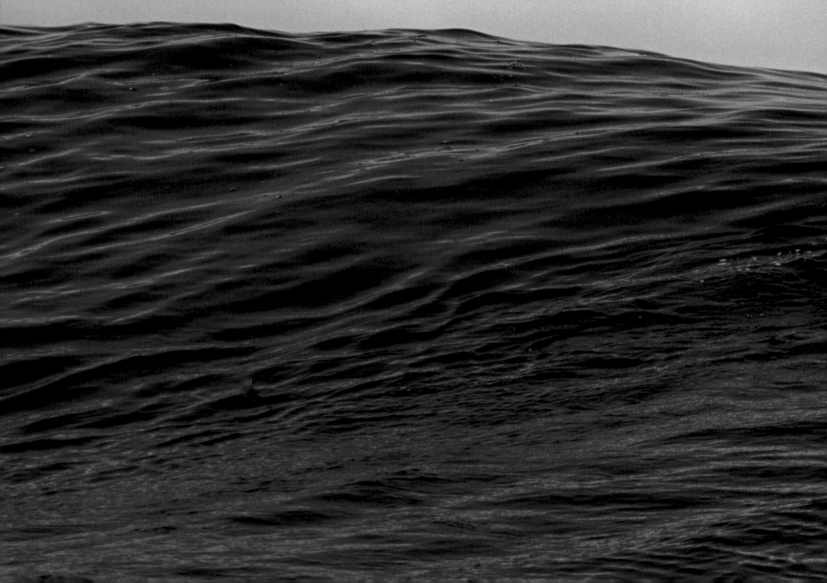

Foreword

In the SPRING of 1963, this guy walked into OLE SURFBOARDS on Bay Boulevard in Seal Beach, California, where I worked as manager Mickey Muñoz's left-hand man. This was in a time when surf shops sold surfboards, period! The use of neoprene wetsuits hadn't yet arrived, and the only other auxiliary income such a retail operation might allow itself to derive came from patching dinged boards. Selling other stuff was considered sissy, nonpurist.

The guy was wearing a madras shirt, black pants, and brown leather shoes with white socks. He turned out to be a salesman, and he wanted us to carry his new brand of surf trunks called "Hang Ten." We flat out refused to even consider selling surf trunks to our customers, and he eventually went down the highway a few miles to Huntington Beach and successfully talked Jack Hokanson into carrying his trunks. The parable to this story is, Ole Surfboards ceased operations some years later while Jack's Surf Shop grew into a multimillion dollar business that sold everything under the sun related to surf and beach. The guy who tried to convince us of what was around the corner was named Duke Boyd. Muñoz and I became lifelong friends with him, but we never bought his trunks. He gave them to us.

Hang Ten was the first commercially produced authentic surf trunk, and the company eventually topped a hundred million dollars a year in sales. Hang Ten also owned the ad space on the back cover of *Surfer* magazine where Duke articulated Hang Ten's relationship with the sport of surfing in ways that other company's couldn't fathom. One of Duke's secrets to success with Hang Ten was that he picked a very graphic logo symbol that represented a high level of skill (and corn) to surfing acolytes. Then he moved the logo from being hidden inside the collar and placed it boldly on the chest; he infused that logo with so much promotion and romance that the name quickly lost it's corn factor and became a household word for surf trunks and raglan-sleeve woven shirts in every color of the rainbow. That was another of Duke's secrets. If you wanted to do volume, you created a branded basic that everyone needed and bought, then got them to buy into your brand's "cool" factor rather than some meaningless mark.

Early in his Hang Ten years, just as *Wide World of Sports* was first flourishing, Duke saw surfing as a potential TV sports subject that was being ignored because it was mis-understood. While managing an apartment in Long Beach to get free rent, he invited all the sport's heroes—Phil Edwards, Dewey Weber, Corky Carroll, Donald Takyama . . . maybe twenty-five to thirty of them—to his apartment to talk them into forming a professional surfers union and present the concept of covering a worldwide series of competitions to network television. As a group, they found the idea interesting, but no one pursued it.

While Duke was building Hang Ten, his friend Dick Graham was serving as publisher of Peterson's *International Surfing* maga-zine, which was floundering in second place behind the seminal *Surfer* magazine. Graham hired Duke as managing editor to help create authentic content and to merchandise that title like he did his clothing brand. Graham was a jock and body surfer, and Duke was hooked into the surf scene, so Duke started going to his beach buddies at Huntington Pier near where he lived, recruited them as test riders for his surf trunks, well before anyone had team riders, and started Graham running articles on and by those underground heroes. That strategy worked in both cases.

Around the same time, Duke was running an advertising agency for surf companies he was friendly with that didn't compete with Hang Ten—amongst them, Dive & Surf Wetsuits, for whom he created the Body Glove name and logo; Greg Noll Surfboards, for whom he helped develop the most unique and popular, totally anarchistic surfboard ad campaign in the history of the sport, for Mickey Dora's Da Cat Model; and Bing Surf-boards during its late 1960s transition from long-nose riders to the shorter, more-spontaneous "pocket rockets."

While designing and merchandising Hang Ten, Duke created and developed the Golden Breed brand for Hang Ten's primary men's and boy's licensee and his dear friend and mentor Robert McAllister; worked with surf filmmaker Dale Davis to make and merchandise the film of the same title; with Hawai'ian surfing great George Downing, created the Objective Scoring System for judging surf contests; and with 1960s–1970s surf

Duke Boyd.

all-star Jeff Hakman, created the experi-mental Expression Session anti-surf contest exhibition format.

Eventually, Duke and his better-business-half partner Doris Moore sold Hang Ten and Duke moved to Aspen, Colorado, where he lived on Woody Creek down the way from Hunter S. Thompson, skied Aspen mountain fast with Chart House restaurant founder Joey Cabell and their friend Tommy Lee, and explored life a bit, attending EST seminars and thinking about what to do next. "Next" turned out to be taking a red-hot grassroots surfboard brand, Light-ning Bolt, and licensing it for surf wear. It was partially a test, to see if Hang Ten had meant he really knew something unusual, or was it just luck. It, too, succeeded, and he realized it was probably a healthy dose of both.

Much of the surf industry's ultimate growth into a multi-billion-dollar category has been based on principles of brand merchandising and retail that Duke originated back in the 1960s, using off-the-cuff ideas and seat-of-the-pants logic of his own and of surfers around him who he alone bothered to listen to, all based on applications of the real stoke of surfing that drove the underpinnings of the surf marketplace. You had to be a surfer to know the feeling, and Duke was a surfer.

Duke has always urged those around him to be all they can be, myself included. The ultimate romantic when it comes to amplifying the inner qualities of riding waves that become so compelling to all surfers, Duke has always been taken by the rich human pageantry of the surfing individuals that makes up the core sport. He has always wanted to take a stab at chroni-cling in book form those hard-to-touch human qualities that make the sport eccentric and wonderful.

In this day and age, the realities of book publishing tend to compress big ideas to fit within such practical boundaries as price point and time schedules. If Duke was unrestricted by that reality, his passion for the subject would demand that this tome measure three by four feet and contain several hundred poster-sized pages, painstakingly printed on the heaviest sheet, featuring thrillingly huge and impactful reproductions of the most incredible surf photos ever taken, accompanied by genre-defining essays by surfing's most eloquent writers, each edition coming with a custom, handcrafted teakwood floor stand. While reality does make it something we can conveniently hold in our hands, this book attempts to realize the very same aspiration, to touch the soul of surfing. That's always been Duke's dream.

~ Steve Pezman
Steve Pezman is the publisher of The Surfer's Journal.

Introduction

Legendary Surfriders of the Twentieth Century

As the twentieth-century surfing generation was forming around the world, I was fortunate to be searching for surf, riding shotgun, living the lifestyle of a dedicated surf bum, and all the while sharing waves with the future icons of surfing. Some of them were older than me, pioneer surfers, but most were hot young surf gremmies of the 1950s to the 1970s, the soon-to-be master shapers, surf photographers, film directors, and magazine editors of the awakening surfing world. All were young and enticed, addicted, and devoted to riding waves. Their priorities were surf, surf again, eat, sleep, and sex—in that order.

While attending Long Beach State College during the early 1960s, I joined up with a clothing manufacturer, Doris Moore, and formed Hang Ten, the first nationally distributed grassroots surfwear company. By way of my Hang Ten affiliation, I was slipped a kind of stealthy, "backstage" surf pass that allowed me to participate as one of the emerging surf community. This lucky draw in life gave me the opportunity to enter the lineup and watch the surfing hierarchy from up close—the best seat in the house. Yes, I'm a fan, and it was a surf adventure you can only dream about.

Coming into being long ago in prehistory Polynesia, then migrating to the Hawai'ian Islands, surfing was the sport of the *Ali'i* (royalty). When the missionaries arrived, surfing was discouraged, even suppressed, until it was resurrected at the turn of the twentieth century. Duke Kahanamoku, a pure Hawai'ian, known as the father of surfing, became the emissary of Aloha, spreading surfing around the world during his travels.

Like seafaring sailors and mountain men before them, surfers grew into a breed quite distinctive from "normal" society. They first gathered along the world's beaches where places with good waves and pleasant living became "surf ghettos"—or better, brotherhoods—of international surfing aficionados. During that period, the surfing movement became recognized as an original expression of human endeavor—a lifestyle blended with a challenging art form making for a meaningful life philosophy.

When I first began surfing in the late 1950s, there were few surfriders. A lot of those surfers, as well as others who followed, are featured in this book. Many of them, I am proud to say, are lifelong surfing buddies and friends whom I have surfed with. I became aware of the others through my travels, and of course the "coconut wireless."

"With a little help from my friends," I have selected the surfers herein for a variety of reasons; my guiding theory being the distinctive, individual surfer's role played in the mosaic that was the twentieth century's surfing society.

Sadly, I could not squeeze in everyone who deserves to be in this book. Those featured are merely a sample from the rich human pool that resides at the heart of my surfing life. All are my heroes and all are legendary surfriders of the twentieth century.

Andy Irons takes wing above the crest in 2002.

PIONEER SURFRIDERS

SURFING'S RECORDED HISTORY dates back to Captain Cook's first written observation in 1777. Since the recording of his insightful words, there has been an increasing body of literature dedicated to explaining the essence of wave riding. However, the more colorful and undoubtedly richest modes have been verbal—the passing of lore from generation to generation via "talking story" and the coconut wireless.

Early drawings and etchings from Captain Cook's voyages to the Sandwich Isles recorded men and women cavorting on short planks in near-shore waves of moderate size. Their Polynesian ancestors are believed to be the original watermen and waterwomen, the original surfers.

Around the middle of the twentieth century, wave riding became increasingly noticed by a curious public. The population of surfers began to grow as the recreational value of surfing became more evident; surfboards became more accessible, lighter and easier to use; and a surf media developed to fan the flames of surf stoke. By the early 1960s, the sport had grown from thousands to millions, surf magazines were starting up, surf movies were touring beach-town high school auditoriums around the country, and new regional tribes of surf-feverish wave riders searched the coasts for surf.

Decades later, the teenagers of the 1960s have become the aging surf historians of the new millennium, intent on preserving the endearing times of their surfing youth, documented in super-8 home movies, old photos and magazines, and the recollections of the early surf pioneers.

Those pioneers were drawn to the ocean and enticed with everything above and below it. They inquisitively observed the rhythm of the tides, became able to predict seasonal arctic and southern hemisphere storms, became sensitized to wave and wind direction, and the effect of reefs, bars, points, and man-made piers and jetties on wave shapes. Observing the ocean as a daily ritual made the habits of the ocean become ingrained in their blood. Eventually, those most skilled in the ocean arts became regarded as "watermen" and "waterwomen" and, by being so in sync, were revered surf riders as well.

Over time, the pioneers of surfing created specialized surfboard designs for the various wave conditions they encountered. As the boards became more refined, so did the riding of them. In the earlier years of surfing, the surfboards were heavy and ponderous. As they became lighter and the shapes and use of fins more understood, surfing morphed from the rider standing on the board and letting it take him to shore, to much freer, inventive, spontaneous forms of personal expression and increasingly acute positioning on the wave. Our world of oceans and seas, once a relative mystery, is now known to encompass many, many rideable surf breaks, each offering as individual an experience as does each successive wave at each break. The surfers who have explored and opened this world were committed, proud, skilled, and original.

Surfing today is fortunate to have these legendary surfing icons, all pioneer surf riders of the twentieth century.

Duke Kahanamoku, the father of surfing.

Duke Kahanamoku
The Father of Surfing

The emerging world of surfriding struck it rich when it realized and recognized Hawai'ian Duke Kahanamoku as its father of surfing. If any surfer was the embodiment of the ideals and virtues of pure free-surfing, the Duke was that surfer. Kahanamoku was a gentleman both in and out of the surf, and he endorsed sharing the waves, the camaraderie that is intertwined within the sport, and the pure joy that is at the heart of surfriding.

Kahanamoku, by way of example, spread Hawai'i's "Aloha spirit" throughout the surfing world. He had a humble manner and sense of humor that was pure ethnic Hawai'ian, setting the stage for surfing's basic philosophy. The art of Hawai'ian surfing was then, and is now, a unique message to an unsettled world. At its base it says, surfing equals the Aloha spirit. In free-surfing, no one wins, no one loses, for there are other endeavors, other games that can serve that purpose.

Upon his return from the 1912 Olympics in Stockholm, Sweden, Duke introduced surfriding and its ideals to America by way of the East Coast, then the West Coast, and later Australia. Hawai'i's gift of Aloha by way and through Duke Kahanamoku International Surf Exhibitions planted the seeds of an enduring ideal philosophy. Kahanamoku was an all-around waterman and included canoes and bodysurfing. His surfing skill lent more to riding the bigger waves off Waikiki, Oahu, with longer boards. The "talk story" tale about Duke riding the fabled "Kings Surf," a huge wave off Diamond Head, all the way to the beach at the Royal Hawai'ian Hotel has never been disputed and is aggrandized. Duke Kahanamoku is truly the father of surfing.

"You know, there are so many waves coming in all the time, you don't have to worry about that. Take your time— wave come. Let the other guys catch another one."

—*Duke Kahanamoku*

The world's first surfing hero, Duke Kahanamoku stands with a towering *olo* surfboard at Waikiki Beach.

Alexander Hume Ford
Founder of the Outrigger Canoe Club

Alexander Hume Ford loved Hawai'i, and he loved surfing. Upon arriving in the American Territory of Hawai'i in 1907, he checked out the surf, made himself a plank, and went surfing. Ford practiced every day until he mastered it and was capable of riding with the local natives.

Early on, Ford recognized that surfing had been stunted by the missionaries during the previous century, and by founding the Outrigger Canoe Club in 1908, he took it upon himself to promote the Islands' surf culture for the purpose of "reviving and preserving the ancient Hawai'ian sport of surfing on boards and outrigger canoes."

Alexander Hume Ford was Hawai'i's—and in effect the surfing world's—vanguard in promoting surfing. As he was eulogized in *The Honolulu Advertiser* in 1945, Ford was "the livest wire of all the Pacific commonwealth." *Bishop Museum*

Charles "Snow" McAlister
The Father of Australian Surfing

Charles McAlister, a.k.a. "Snow," was blown away when Hawai'ian Olympic champion and legendary surfer Duke Kahanamoku exhibited his surfing prowess at Manly Beach, Australia. Snow was 10 and clearly impressed. He hung up his ironing board and began building his own board by copying Duke's.

In 1926, Snow made a winning run for the Australian National Titles and took three in a row, the last one narrowly with a headstand to the beach.

Snow made surfing his life's story, keeping involved throughout his life by authoring surf columns for *Surfing World* magazine, supporting Bob Evans with his touring surf movies, and co-founding the Australian Surfriders Association.

Recognized as the father of Australian surfing, Charles McAlister was born in 1904 and inducted into the Australian Surfing Hall of Fame in 1985, honoring a legendary surfrider for surfing 78 years.

Bob Evans
Australian Pioneer Surfrider

By all reliable accounts, Bob Evans was a formidable "good surfrider," one of Australia's best during the 1950s. It's also fair to say that, in some ways, Evans' multitasking surf culture pursuits overshadowed his surfing skills. Undaunted or not interested, but never looking back, Bob took off into the Australian surfing world's bevy of opportunities full-on. He loved it, influenced it, shaped it, then recorded its awakening through his publication, *Surfing World* magazine, and his core 16mm films were devoted to discovering what was then a new world called surfing.

To fulfill the Aussie surf culture story, he tied it together with an unprecedented organization, the Australian Surfriders Association, Australia's first nationwide surf group.

In 1987, Bob Evans was brought on board with the Australian Surfing Hall of Fame.

Paul Strauch estimated that Albert "Rabbit" Kekai, who started his surfing career in 1925, rode more than a million waves at Queens over his lifetime.

Albert "Rabbit" Kekai
The Legend

Albert Kekai was known as "Rabbit" because in high school he could run the 100-yard dash in 10 seconds flat when the world record at the time was 9.3 seconds, held by Mel Patton. An outstanding athlete from the South Shore of Oahu, Rabbit's surfing was so far in advance of the other surfers of the 1930s and 1940s that icon surfer Matt Kivlin, visiting from Malibu, admiringly recognized Rabbit as "light years ahead of anybody." Rabbit was famous for his working of the Waikiki waves, usually at Queens, by maneuvering his board up and down the face, then stalling and running to the nose. Arguably, Rabbit was surfing's first "hotdogger."

Rabbit started his surfing career at the age of five and was luckily a protégé of the father of surfing, Duke Kahanamoku. Rabbit won the Makaha International surfing contest on Oahu's West Shore in 1956 at the age of 35. He continued winning surfing contests throughout his long surfing life until the age of 79. *Longboard Magazine* said of Albert Kekai: "Rabbit is the living link to surfing's entire modern history."

A twentieth-century legend, Rabbit was inducted into the *International Surfing* Hall of Fame in 1991, and in 2001 he was given a plaque on the Huntington Beach Surfing Walk of Fame.

Lorrin "Whitey" Harrison
Pioneer California Waverider

Lorrin Harrison, also called "Whitey," is the kind of core surfer that aficionados write books about. Whitey was a real surfer right down to the coconut palm hat he wore when he was surfing at Doheny, California.

Whitey was born in 1913 almost a full century ago, when his family would go to Laguna Beach, California, by horse and wagon. At 12 years of age, he began his love affair with surfing and was in on the pioneering of San Onofre, California's, Waikiki Beach, in 1933. The same year, Whitey won the California Pacific Coast Surf Riding Championships.

In between mainland adventures, Whitey stowed away twice on a cruise ship to Hawai'i and got caught twice but was allowed to stay in Hawai'i the second time. During the late 1930s, Whitey was among those that pioneered the North Shore of Oahu, while finding that Hawai'i's Aloha spirit fit into his ideals of what a surfer's life was supposed to be about. That's where the coconut hat comes from.

Whitey Harrison started surfing in 1925 when he was 12 years old and kept on surfing until 1993— 78 years of staying wet. *Bev Morgan*

By organizing, exploring, and shaping, Wally Froiseth became a major influence in Hawai'i's surfing history.
Walter Hoffman

Wally Froiseth
Inconspicuous Pioneer Surfrider

Hawai'i's Wally Froiseth was surfing's inconspicuous pioneer waverider during the 1930s. Methodically, as a young surfer, he set about quietly involving himself in all aspects of the sport during surfing's most formative years in Hawai'i. At eight years of age, Froiseth, while surfing at Waikiki Beach, fortuitously fell under the influence of the legendary surf icon Tom Blake. In 1937, armed with a need to improve their surfing mobility, Wally along with buddies John Kelly and Fran Heath, three very frustrated inventors, chopped with an axe on Heath's redwood surfboard so that it wouldn't "slide ass" by narrowing the tail. This gave it a gunlike silhouette. Wally dubbed the innovation, the "Hot Curl" surfboard.

During that period, Froiseth and Kelly set out for the West Side of Oahu to first explore the surf treasure of Makaha Beach and later the ominous North Shore. During the 1940s, 13-year-old George Downing, soon to be Hawai'i's legendary big-wave surfrider, came under Wally's wing. Together, they discovered and surfed Laniakea on the North Shore in 1946 and later Maui's Honolua Bay in 1947. These were exciting times for surfing's evolution.

Wally was an original member of the Waikiki Surf Club, which ultimately became the first sponsor of the Makaha International surf contest in 1954. Froiseth won the Makaha in 1959 and then turned to directing that contest, which by that time had become recognized as the mecca of all surf contests during the 1950s and 1960s. The following year, to round out his surfing trade, Wally became the head judge of the Duke Kahanamoku Invitational contests in 1965 and 1966.

Wally Froiseth earned a deserved reputation among the surfing aficionados of the era as the surfer behind the scenes, a dedicated master of big waves who was viewed as surfing's inconspicuous pioneer.

Richard "Buffalo" Keaulana

Buffalo and Sons: Rusty and Brian

Born in 1935, Richard Keaulana, is a full-blooded Hawai'ian surfrider affectionately nicknamed "Buffalo" because of his reddish curly hair. As a young boy in 1940, Buff began his surfing career at Waikiki Beach then moved with his family to Makaha on the leeward side of Oahu. There, Buffalo began a Hawai'ian surfing legacy that extended over more than a half century that included winning the 1968 Makaha International contest and placing seven times in the event from 1957 to 1965. Considered to be a "natural," he taught himself to switch stance so that he could face the wave at Makaha, enabling him always to be in the critical spot on the wave and to increase his edge in the Makaha contests.

Buffalo has two sons following in his wake. Brian is a world renowned, all-around waterman with extraordinary skills that range from paddle-in big wave riding, free-diving, sailboarding, canoe surfing, and tow-in surfing at Jaws. Rusty is a big-wave surfrider who has also won three longboard world championships and placed fifth in the 1991 Eddie Aikau Memorial at Waimea Bay.

Keaulana family members have starred in the surf movies of their respective eras and gained the admiration of those surfing aficionados who have observed the great surfers of the twentieth century.

The Makaha Buffalo Big Board Classic was started by the Keaulana family in 1997, and it has grown to include all kinds of traditional Hawai'ian ocean games topped off with an old-fashioned local beach party.

In 1972, Buffalo Keaulana was honored with a statue placed at the Waianae Public Library near the family's home on the west side of Oahu.

Richard "Buffalo" Keaulana was a legendary pioneer Hawai'ian surfer who was instrumental in establishing the West Side surf spot Makaha. He was also a consistent contestant in the Makaha International contest, winning the event in 1960.

Brian Keaulana has the respect of the surfing world for his expert skills in all things that pertain to surfing, including paddle-in and tow-in big-wave riding, surf canoeing, and bodysurfing. *Warren Bolster*

Rusty Keaulana is Hawai'i's three-time world champion longboarder who also took a respectful fifth in the Quiksilver in memory of Eddie Aikau Big Wave Contest held at Waimea Bay.

Pete Peterson
All-Around Waterman, Surfer, and Paddler

Pete Peterson was a private person, prone to humble interaction. He was born in 1913 and started surfing in Santa Monica, California, in 1921 when he was eight years old. Peterson was a classic example of the era's sportsmanship when it came to bragging about anything. There wasn't any dancing in the end zones or any type of showing off. A self-congratulatory attitude simply was not cool.

Standing about 6 feet, 2 inches, lean and strong, but not imposing, Peterson made his early mark by lifeguarding in California and showing his passion for surfing. In the days of lifeguarding, the skills of swimming, paddling, and surfing were considered essential. Peterson was exemplary in these fields, and in the 1930s and 1940s he set out to earn a master's reputation as an enduring paddler, winning contest after contest in the sprint categories as well as in the open sea. His swimming prowess was evident when he made the first team of lifeguards in Santa Monica in 1932. For more than a decade, Peterson gained an admirable reputation for his lifeguard rescue work. He was twice the winner of the coveted Pacific Coast Guard Championship.

Surfing was Peterson's love. He surfed competitively in the early days of the California amateur contests. He won the Pacific Coast Surfriding Championships four times and won the trophy in the 1966 tandem category. In 1964 and 1966, he took the tandem division at the Huntington Beach, California, United States Surfing Championship and the Makaha International Championship in Hawai'i. Tandem surfing was Peterson's specialty.

Pete Peterson, a legendary waterman, surfer, board builder, swimmer, and paddler was inducted into *International Surfing* magazine's Hall of Fame in 1966.

Pete Peterson was the master tandem champion during the twentieth century, winning six major ranked tandem surfing contests after winning the Pacific Coast Surfriding Championship four times during the 1930s and 1940s. Pete's tandem partner here was Berrie Boehne.
Ron Stoner

Jack "Bluey" Mayes was six years old in 1928 when he began surfing at Bondi Beach, Australia. Bluey gained fame as Australia's foremost waverider by riding a 15-foot hollow board he called the Golden Hawk.

Jack "Bluey" Mayes
Stylish Australian Switch-Footer Surfrider

For about fifteen years during the 1940s and mid-1950s, Jack "Bluey" Mayes was considered one of Australia's best surfriders. Bluey, who of course was a redhead, started out surfing on his mom's ironing board when he was a grommet of six years of age. Over the years, he graduated to his 15-foot Golden Hawk. In 1956, when the South Bay lifeguards from California, headed by legendary surfer Greg Noll, dropped by with their revolutionary Malibu boards, Bluey found his niche. The "Mal" was just what he needed for his next step. Bluey, a switch-footer, could now freely maneuver with style—which he had a lot of!

An acknowledged showoff, Bluey nevertheless was an accredited "good surfer" with a favorable following along Australia's East Coast.

Considered an Australian surfing icon, Bluey was featured in a 1985 television documentary titled *The History of Australian Surfing*.

Woody Brown opened up the Windansea surf break in Southern California before joining up with Hawai'ian legendary surfers Fran Heath, Wally Froiseth, and John Kelly to pioneer Makaha and the North Shore with the newly created Hot Curl board. *Woody Brown family archive*

Woodbridge "Woody" Brown

Legendary Explorer

Among his amazing legendary accomplishments in the 1940s, Woodbridge "Woody" Brown was already big-wave exploring on Hawai'i's North Shore. Brown started his career in 1936, building his first surfboard and then becoming the first to ride the famous Windansea surf spot in California. From there, he sailed to Hawai'i and took up with Hawai'ian surfers Wally Froiseth and John Kelly. At the time, the Hot Curl surfboard was just being fine-tuned, so it was perfect timing for Woody to take it to the North Shore and Makaha on an exploring quest for new surf spots.

On a historic day in surfing lore in 1943, Dickie Cross and Brown went out at Sunset Beach, Oahu, to ride the 10-foot surf that had just come up. Once out, the surf surprisingly jumped up to 25 feet and began closing out. Both surfers had to paddle down to Waimea Bay to try to get to shore only to find that it too was closing out across the bay.

With sea waves ranging in the 40-foot-plus category, it eliminated the route to shore and safety. Sadly, Cross drowned trying to make it to the beach, while Woody was luckily swept in to safety. His near drowning at Waimea Bay affected him to the point that he never surfed the North Shore again. The legend of Waimea as unrideable and too dangerous was thus created.

John "Wheels" Williams
Australian Pioneer Waverider, Photographer, Journalist

John Williams, an Australian surfrider known as "Wheels," got his nickname after a hair-raising ride with British race-car driver Stirling Moss.

In 1957, Wheels got the bug and took up surfing at his home break, Bondi Beach. He was an eager 17 years old. From there, Wheels began communicating with John Severson, and the two found mutual interests. Wheels was soon sending *Surfer* magazine photographs and articles depicting the then-mysterious land Down Under, and soon also barnstorming the East Coast showing John's surf movies.

Although Wheels was a "good surfer" and did well in competing in Europe during his travels, including winning the 1965 European Championship, he nevertheless felt that professional surfing changed the sport. "It brought a little bit of ugliness into the water for quite a while." For Wheels, "Camaraderie is what surfing is all about."

After witnessing Rabbit Kekai surf at Waikiki, Matt Kivlin developed his interpretation of performance surfing at Malibu, a style that Kemp Aaberg called "cruising." *Joe Quigg*

Matt Kivlin
Pioneer Malibu Style Master

Matt Kivlin was the style master of Malibu long before Gidget went to Hollywood and surfing became famous. Back when the classic pointbreak was just being explored, Kivlin was perfecting his style there, a style that would be the envy of Malibu surfriders that were soon to follow. Kivlin's style was to surf close to the curl with a smooth, no-frills approach, much like Hawai'ian Rabbit Kekai, the legendary surfer of Queens, Oahu's classic South Shore surf spot. Mickey Dora was one of Malibu's legendary surfriders who keyed off Matt's mannerism, leading to a cool style that was Malibu.

Kivlin partnered up with Joe Quigg to make surfboards that morphed into the lighter Malibu Chip. Later, he also hooked up briefly with Bob Simmons. Although Matt never got the board-building acclaim he deserved (having been overshadowed by Quigg and Simmons), he did a thriving stealth surfboard business. All said, Matt Kivlin, the gentleman surfer of Malibu, was its first style master.

The
GOLDEN
AGE

THE GOLDEN ERA OF SURFING

ranged between 1950 and 1970 with a little overlap on both sides of the era. It was a magical time to be a surfer in the world as things were dramatically and quickly changing. Adventure was in the air with siren calls to join the surfers and see the world, surfari to the Hawai'ian Islands, trip out to Down Under, search for surf at Cape Saint Francis, get wet, get stoked, and go surfing. It was all good fun, exciting, new, and magical.

It also was a time to challenge Waimea Bay . . . for courageous pioneer surfers to ride big Makaha without skegs on their new Hot Curl boards . . . while the Malibu Chip was being introduced to the point and the Velzy pig was changing everything. The surfing life was good—and getting better. Phil Edwards showed us some style, Mickey Dora danced lightly like Da Cat, Dale Velzy became the iconic image of a core salty surfer.

We all went to the surf movies, snapped bottlecaps, hooted, and dreamed of riding the Banzai Pipeline. Bud Browne, Bruce Brown, and John Severson, along with Greg MacGillivray and Jim Freeman, showed us how much pure fun surfing really was.

Of course, Severson saw it coming. He looked at surfing as it was emerging from the vacuum and gave it an image and a language with his magazines. Then he followed up with original surf photography all the while documenting its historical moods, changes, and adventures.

The board builders went wild with the reshaping of the surfboards, then moving smartly from the heavy redwood sleds to hollow boxes to lighter balsa boards—and then to the discovery of the easy-to-shape motherlode, foam. Now, all the boards would eventually go light, lighter, and then short and lighter. Surfboards evolved from the Model T plank to the 911 Porsche shortboard in two decades.

We hung ten and swung our turns with style and ease. Then, we all almost in unison changed our attitudes in midstream with the urging of our Aussie brothers. We went radical, we ripped, we tore, and we explored every pocket, every tube, and tripped out on every inch of the waves, big or small. The Banzai Pipeline went from "Oh my God, it's too dangerous!" to "Hey, this is a cake walk!"

It seems obvious now, but surfing went into overhaul during this golden age. And after a major makeover, it emerged like a spanking new baby, ready for go.

John Severson
Pioneer, Seer, Surfrider

John Severson's contribution to the surfing world is unmatched. In fact, surfing owes Severson a standing ovation. Through his foresight, Severson gave surfers stature. He did it by telling the world about the emerging surf culture through the founding of his periodical *Surfer*, his filmmaking, and his interpretive artistry.

Through *Surfer* magazine, John communicated the ideals of surfers to other surfers. It was "surfer speak"—a different dialect of sorts, unique to the coconut wireless membership. With Severson's insight and guidance, *Surfer* became known as "the bible" because of its loyalty to surfers' hard-core values.

John portrayed the surfing culture through his involvement and observation of the lifestyle. *Surfer* magazine was his instrument for describing what was at the time the dropped-out, vagabond surfer, who in politically correct social circles was just a "beach bum." Severson's early photography, insightful prose, and artistic illustration of the real surfer gave recognition and stature to an emerging exclusive cult of watermen. Severson started with a vacuum and filled it with an endorsement of a new sect of humanity that was creatively framed in beautiful ocean waves and faraway secret spots. Severson recognized and recorded the rag-tag barefoot, pre-Vietnam, long-haired, fur coat fashion that was unique to surfing and had come from the racks of the Salvation Army. It was the core of the 1960s revolution: the laid-back lifestyle, the beach clothing and designs all prior to the California hippies. Severson absorbed and deciphered all this and then shared it with the surfing world.

John Severson was a seer, a pioneer, a champion, an insightful writer, a master surfrider, magazine editor, a publisher of historical surfing books, a pioneer filmmaker, and a world-class interpretive artist.

He did it all, and surfing is beholden to him.

A champion international surfrider, a visionary, an artist, and a notable writer, editor, and publisher, John Severson carefully guided and recorded for perpetuity the 1960s surfing revolution. *John Severson collection*

THE SURFER MAGAZINE

A John Severson Production

"Every genre has to start somewhere, and it started with me. Maybe I could have done a better job, but at least it had a sense of humor, it had a lot of color, and it represented the culture of surfing. Best I could do, starting out in a vacuum."

—John Severson

Early on, Conrad Canha was Hawai'i's hottest tuberider and gained a notable reputation for taking heavy lip hits and miraculously not being wiped out. *John Severson*

Conrad Canha

Premier Hawai'ian Hot-dogger and Tuberider

Conrad Canha was one of Hawai'i's original hot-doggers and a leader of snap turns, walking the board, and riding the nose. He was also able to withstand powerful broken waves and was hard to knock off his board. Conrad was famous for surviving almost certain wipe-outs by keeping a low center of gravity and applying pure determination. Yes, he was a "good surfer!"

Ala Moana Bowl was Conrad's proving ground for his then-inventive style of tuberiding, but it was his surf experience in big waves at Makaha that paved the way for his championship success in the 1956 Makaha International. The next year, Conrad continued his winning ways by traveling to South America and winning both the small and big wave events of the 1957 Peru International surf competition.

True to his surfer roots, Conrad Canha's core surfing philosophy put his surfing first, which translated into doing only as much work as necessary and as much surfing as possible.

Bernard "Midget" Farrelly was the first world-champion surfer. He led the Australian competitive surge into international waters by winning the 1962 Makaha International contest in Hawai'i before taking the 1964 World Championship title in Manly Beach, Sydney, Australia. *Alby Falzon*

Bernard "Midget" Farrelly
Premiere Surfriding Champion

Bernard Farrelly, a.k.a. "Midget," is recognized internation-ally as the first world champion by winning its inaugural crown in 1964 at Manly Beach, Sydney, Australia.

Midget, Australia's surfing patriarch, was born in Oz in 1944 and started his surfing pursuits at the early age of six. Accruing a winning string of championships over an eight-year time period, he was considered to be one of the elite international competitive surfers in the world.

In 1962, Farrelly won the Makaha International contest on Oahu's West Shore, a feat that had major game-changing results. First, the Makaha International was at the time "The Contest" to win if you were to be recognized in the emerging competitive surf scene. Second, it was in Hawai'i, on the world famous Makaha Beach, the home locals' beach of Hawai'i's premier surfers. Coming from Down Under to win at Makaha meant that you had to be really, really good in order to impress the Hawai'ian judges.

When Midget was awarded the Makaha championship, the doors opened up immediately for truly international surf competition.

Midget was a strong supporter of the Australian Surfriding Association and the International Surfing Federation. He appeared in several surf movies, including John Severson's *Pacific Vibrations*. Midget won his share of accolades by getting the most Aussie votes in the California-based *International Surfing* magazine Hall of Fame awards and was inducted in 1986 into the Australian Surfing Hall of Fame.

Midget Farrelly was a longboard stylist in the classic tradition of Paul Strauch, Billy Hamilton, and Phil Edwards.

Jeff Hakman
Mr. Sunset

When the winter swells arrived, Jeff Hakman would sit inconspicuously in the middle of the pack at Honolua Bay on Maui, quietly biding his time. When the sets began to show on the horizon, Jeff would wait like a cat eyeing a mouse. The first wave would arrive with the pack scrambling for position. Hakman didn't move. Then the second wave would appear, and more scrambling would take place. As the pack began to vie for their spots and the second wave of the set moved in, Jeff would lazily and sneakily move away to a calm spot where the third wave had not yet formed. There he would sit and wait in the prime slot without having to battle for position. Then, all alone, Hakman would take off and slip into the best of the Honolua set waves, smiling all the way.

Jeff was considered to be a master surfer who as a teenager was already a high-profile, notable North Shore surfer. As a child star phenomenon at the age of 12, he began to earn his reputation as "Mr. Sunset."

Jeff took away a bundle of trophies in his day, winning the first Pipeline Masters in 1971, the Duke Kahanamoku Invitational in 1970 and 1971, the Hang Ten American Pro and the Gunston 500 in 1973, and he came in second to Reno Abellira at the 30-foot-plus Waimea Bay Smirnoff contest in 1974. He completed his surf contest career as a non-Aussie with a win at Bell's Beach in Victoria, Australia.

As a pioneer big-wave surfrider, Jeff won the 1966 *International Surfing* magazine Hall of Fame award and was the subject of the book *Mr. Sunset* by Phil Jarratt, which was about his life as a master surfer of the twentieth century.

Jeff Hakman earned his surfing reputation at Sunset Beach, yet he was equally adept anywhere on the North Shore. Here, Hakman has positioned himself on an ominous but perfect 25-foot Waimea wave. Just another day at the bay.

Rusty Miller's legacy will long be featured on the pages of surfing history with this classic photograph of him making the drop at Sunset Beach on Oahu's North Shore. *Dr. Don James*

Rusty Miller

Master of Sunset

Sometimes one great picture can do more for your reputation than a decade of winning contests.

Rusty Miller was photographed by Dr. Don James, riding a classic Sunset Beach pitching wave that framed his power descent. It was picturesque water shot that so summed up the excitement of surfing that even a nonsurfer from Kansas could appreciate it. Hamm's Beer used the shot for a billboard advertising campaign, forever emblazoning Rusty in the pages of surfing history.

Born in La Jolla, California, in 1943, Miller took up surfing when he was 10, living in Encinitas and surfing Swamis. A sterling competitor, Miller took part in the West Coast championships, placing second in 1961 and fourth in 1962. He finished up his California competition pursuits as the 1965 points leader in the United States Surfing Association rankings.

While living in Kauai, Miller was an acknowledged big-wave rider at the time the Hawai'ian Islands' surf was still being pioneered.

Rusty eventually moved Down Under to Sydney, Australia, and in the 1970s to Byron Bay, where he teaches surfing.

John "L. J." Richards

Legendary Surfrider

John Richards, known by friends as Little John or "L. J.," was a classic example of his era's no-frills stylish method of surfriding. L. J. began surfing at the age of 13 in 1952. Eleven years later, the Oceanside regular-foot slipped quietly into the West Coast Championships held at Huntington Beach and slipped out with a first place trophy.

In those days, the West Coast Championships were considered to be America's premier surfing events, alongside the Makaha International contest on Oahu. Placing that coveted trophy on his mantle, L. J. was invited in 1964 to take part in the first ever World Surfing Championships being held Down Under in Sydney. Upon arriving, L. J. found the Aussie surf aficionados were putting on an enthusiastic reception. "We were treated like movie stars," he noted. L. J. finished fourth in the world behind Midget Farrelly, Mike Doyle, and Joey Cabell.

After appearing in a series of Bruce Brown's vintage surf movies in the 1950s and 1960s, L. J. was inducted into the International Surfing Hall of Fame in 1991.

John "L. J." Richards has quietly and steadily gone about his surfing lifestyle without fanfare, winning along the way the 1963 West Coast Championship and placing fourth in the World Championship in 1964. *Leo Hetzel*

Joey Cabell

Hawai'i's Master International Champion

Joey Cabell likes to be first. He likes to be on the cutting edge. During the wild expanding 1960s, Cabell and the sport of surfing expanded right along with it. Competitive surfing was *the* happening around the world and Joey was going for it. He took to the international surfing contests like a man on a serious mission and emerged as the decade's finest all-around surfer. A classic example of Cabell's preparation, skill, and concentration was when in 1963, he won both the Makaha International contest at 15- to 18-plus feet, and the Malibu Invitational in waist-high conditions.

When the shortboard revolution overturned the longboard era in 1968, Cabell was on the forefront of the design-shaping edge with his personally shaped board, The White Ghost, an 8-foot, 3-inch precursor of the modern shortboards to come. The White Ghost was designed to fulfill Cabell's theory of picking a line and going full speed in a stance much like the egg posture that the downhill ski-racers were employing at the time. (Cabell was a ski-racer as well.)

In 1964, the California State Legislature formally congratulated Cabell for his earlier win at the Makaha International contest in Hawai'i, and in 1985 *Surfer* magazine pointed to Joey Cabell as one of the 25 surfers whose surfing had changed the sport.

Speaking about the first World Contest held in Australia in 1964, Cabell said, "In the finals I pretty much won the contest, but I did take off on Midget a couple of times, and [judge] Phil Edwards decided this is the time we're going to change all that, so he took me from first place to third place because of my interference on taking off. You've got to realize in my growing up in Hawai'i, there wasn't any wrong with it."

Some claimed that Joey Cabell was the best international all-around competitor during the 1960s. Yet he never took a contest for granted. Joey would prepare with consistent daily workouts both on land and sea. *Warren Bolster*

With the endorsement of notable surf filmmaker Bruce Brown and the peer-driven coconut wireless, Phil Edwards got the well-deserved reputation of being surfing's quintessential power stylist circa 1950–1960. This classic photo was taken by associate editor Bev Morgan especially for the cover of *Surfer*. *Bev Morgan*

Phil Edwards

Style Master

In 1999, Phil Edwards was named by *Surfer* magazine as one of the 25 most influential surfers of the twentieth century. Considered by aficionados to be the best original power stylist of the 1950s, Phil gained international coconut wireless fame by starring in 1950s and 1960s core surf movies and appearing consistently in the surf magazines of the time. Never really a true contest surfer, seeming never to have his heart in it, Edwards eventually passed on serious competition, allowing his free-style power surfing reputation to make his case for greatness.

There were a number of surfers who claimed to have ridden the Banzai Pipeline before Edwards did in 1961. It could be true, but the documented historical evidence points to Bruce Brown's *Surfing Hollow Days*, in which Edwards was filmed riding with his cool signature poise inside the Pipeline tube. With that ride, Brown captured one of surfing's most historical events, and Phil Edwards was memorialized in the annals of surfing lore. In 1966, Phil was inducted by *International Surfing* magazine into the Hall of Fame. Eventually, in 1995, he was awarded his well-deserved plaque on Huntington Beach's Surfing Walk of Fame.

Jack and Mike Haley

Champions

Jack and younger brother Mike Haley were one of several sets of accomplished surfing brothers from Seal Beach, California, in the late 1950s–1960s. They were raised under the tutorage of Lloyd Murray and Robert August, as well as their salty 1940s surfer and Mexico explorer father, Blackie. Their oceanfront house in front of the surf break at 13th Street in Seal provided a gathering place for the local clan, all den-mothered by Blackie's wife, Pat.

Of course, it was Jack who stole a sphinx off the rooftop corner of a Long Beach apartment house and installed it over the beach entry to the August home, prompting for years after, an annual summer celebration that featured the adornment of the figure's nipples with pink paint, accompanied by a keg or two buried in the sand and consumed via surgical tubing straws. *Surfer* magazine founder and surf artist John Severson, who roomed at the August abode while attending Long Beach State, recalls Jack stimulating the surf culture's rebellious penchant for wearing ragged, old fur coats and the like by his attending raucous parties dressed in his own bizarre wardrobe of socially abhorrent thrift store castoffs and Nazi uniform parts.

Jack was unquestionably a great surfer in his era as well as a colorful character, winning the first annual United States Surfing Championship at Huntington Pier in 1959. His little bro Mike took that same crown in 1960. Both were featured in early surf films and magazines.

Mike later married Miss Surf-O-Rama, Sherry Novack, and both tooled around the California surf scene in matching black 1967 Shelby Mustangs. As life progressed, Jack became a successful restaurateur and a real-estate millionaire who bought Frank Sinatra's yacht, while Mike and Sherry started a ladies swimwear company that flourished for a while before dissolving. Still, neither brother ever departed too far from their surfing-based penchant for enjoying an artfully pulled off caper at the expense of those who took themselves too seriously.

Steve Pezman, who authored this sketch, was also a part of the Seal clan.

Mike Haley was always into high fashion in between competition. He was a California surfer who had deep roots in the forming of the golden age era.

With his patented backside soul arch, Captain Jack Haley sets up to shoot the Pier and win the 1959 West Coast Championship. *Bruce Brown*

Mickey Dora
The Dark Knight of Malibu

Mickey Dora was named by *Surfer* magazine as one of the "Most Influential Surfers of the Twentieth Century," which could not be more true. A devilish character and a master of small-wave riding, he was considered to be among the best, if not arguably *the* best surfer at Malibu during the mid-1950s and early 1960s. This was a time when the Point was dominated by the likes of Dewey Weber, Lance Carson, Mickey ("Mongoose") Muñoz, and Kemp Aaberg. Mickey was nicknamed "Da Cat," which was to describe, among other characteristics, Dora's light-footed moves as he would slip through the congested Malibu maze. Dora ruled!

Malibu's surf was first ridden in 1926 when Highway 1 was opened along the California coast. It also created access for soon-to-be surfers to migrate to the South Bay from Los Angeles and the surrounding cities. It didn't take long for the streetwise surfer, Da Cat, to influence the emerging color, character, and reputation of the Malibu surfers. Consequently, California surfers everywhere were eventually affected a little if not a lot.

Da Cat was the epitome of those colorful Malibu surfers. His reputation included being a "good surfer," but he was also famous for mischievousness, admiration, hero worship, thievery, railing against the crowd of Malibu, and hypocritically (with gusto) throwing open the gates to the joy of surfing by being a Hollywood movie extra in *Gidget* in 1959, *Beach Party* in 1963, and *Ride the Wild Surf* in 1964. Da Cat wasn't timid. He pushed, shoved, and swung his board like a sword at any surfer who was unfortunate enough to get in front of him. And still, Da Cat was cool. He had just enough larceny and skill to charm the young and impressionable Malibu surf gremmies.

When Mickey Dora side-slipped out of life in 2002, he was acknowledged throughout the surf world and beyond as a surfing archetype, an anti-hero, and a master small-wave surfer with few equals.

In 1966, when Dora was inducted into the International Surfing Hall of Fame, he wore a tuxedo with Duke Kahanamoku's pareau-print tennis sneakers. As Dora was awarded his plaque posthumously on the Huntington Beach Surfing Walk of Fame, it was noted during the ceremony that Da Cat was probably "up there" giving "the finger" to everybody down here.

Mickey "Da Cat" Dora light-foots it in his fashion-forward, pareau-print, Duke Kahanamoku sneakers during the 1966 International Surfing magazine Hall of Fame awards. *Tom Keck*

Surfing's all-American icon, Mike Doyle could do it all, from mastering big and small waves to tandem surfing and paddling races—while all the time looking like the prototype muscular, tall, tan, 8x10-glossy, smiling beach boy with a surfboard under his arm. Not a bad legacy. *Dick Graham*

Charles "Corky" Carroll was the consummate champion surfer during the golden 1960s. *Dick Graham*

Mike Doyle
All-Around American Waverider

Mike Doyle was twentieth-century surfing's all-around American surfrider. His skills ranged from tandem surfing to paddleboard racing. In the men's surfing championship category, Doyle placed in or won at least five international contests. He got the second spot behind Midget Farrelly in the inaugural World Contest held in 1964 in Australia; he then went on to win the 1968 Duke Kahanamoku Invitational in Hawai'i, and in 1969, he won the Peru International.

A gregarious, good-natured surf star attraction in early surf movies, Doyle stood out as a 6-foot, 2-inch, easy-going, handsome, blonde, smiling, tan, muscular, iconic image for what the world might imagine as the perfect California prototype surfer. He was idolized by younger surfers, with many of them mimicking his style of riding.

Mike Doyle took the top honors in 1964 and 1965 in *Surfer* magazine's prestigious Reader's Poll. In 1966, *International Surfing* magazine's Hall of Fame said he was the best international surfrider of the year.

"When there are waves, I am on it. No coat and tie. I'm not rich, but my life is. Freedom is wealth."

—*Corky Carroll*

Charles "Corky" Carroll
America's Legendary Champion Surfrider

Surfing in the mid- to late 1960s was going to go professional sooner or later. The lazy days of summer with uncrowded waves and sharing the surf with your buddies was coming to an end. The lure of glamour and cash was beginning to call just as Charles "Corky" Carroll matured and the world of professional surfing came into being.

Starting in 1965, Corky won the Laguna Beach Swimwear Masters contest and earned a TV set. Next, he goofy-footed to win $250 at Tom Morey's Invitational Contest (the first professional cash award ever given for a surf event). Carroll went on to work the surf endorsement business by representing Hobie Surfboards (Corky Carroll model), Jantzen swimwear, and Miller Light Beer.

Riding waves was always Corky's true calling. He has always been a hard-core gremmie surfer at heart, and the fact that he went pro was simply to make him enough "surfer money" to keep him wet. It was either that, or he'd have to get a real job.

Corky Carroll won the *Surfer* magazine Readers' Poll in 1967, was inducted into the *Surfing* magazine Hall of Fame in 1996, received a star on the Huntington Beach Surfing Walk of Fame, and is still surfing after all these years.

Kemp Aaberg
Master Stylist of Malibu

When Kemp Aaberg began surfing in Malibu, California, during the *Gidget* era, circa 1955–1959, he started out as a goofy-footer. Terry "Tubesteak" Tracy, the unofficial Malibu beach captain, suggested that Aaberg switch his stance so that he could face the waves, allowing for better maneuvering. Consequently, early in his surf career, Aaberg gained a reputation as a Malibu stylist. This opened the doors for him to co-star in Bruce Brown's first movie, *Slippery When Wet*. In a film by John Severson, Kemp was freeze-framed at Rincon, California, doing a soul arch. That classic pose was memorialized on the pages of *Surfer* as the magazine's iconic logo. Kemp Aaberg was inducted in 1991 to the International Surfing Hall of Fame. Always a humble surfer, he felt genuinely honored to be recognized by his peers. Kemp side-stepped the surfing contest circuit of the time and remained a free-style surfer—the master stylist of Malibu.

Kemp Aaberg had his roots dug deep in the early glory days of Malibu. A master stylist among iconic stylists, Kemp got the nod from his peers. And he could play a mean guitar. *John Severson*

"People over the years have asked me, 'Why do you spend so much time surfing?' It is perhaps one of the most difficult questions for me to answer because surfing is so much a part of my consciousness and lifestyle. It's just part of who I am.

"I love surfing because it leads to so many wonderful experiences: meeting new and interesting people, fun times traveling, learning about the world. Through surfing, I get a great appreciation of what's fulfilling and wholesome in life. Riding waves keeps me fit and feeling vitally alive. I think of surfers as dolphins, an integral part of nature."

—*Kemp Aaberg*

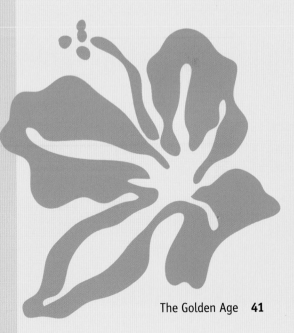

The Golden Age **41**

Lance Carson

Master Noserider of Malibu

Lance Carson was the noseriding artist of Malibu during the late 1950s and early 1960s. Carson ruled the nose. Drawing out deep turns, he would next move smoothly to the nose of the board and then hang out. He was good—a master surfrider during Malibu's magical era.

Lance and Mickey Dora were the top guns of Malibu along with Kemp Aaberg. They set the bar for all the local surfers in "The Pit" and for visitors alike. It was a classic demonstration of surfing with style by Carson and the masters of Malibu that will forever be idolized by the aficionados of that world-class pointbreak.

John Milius, the director and screenwriter of the Hollywood release *Big Wednesday*, based one of the characters in the film on Carson's persona, which was played by surfrider and actor Jan Michael Vincent. The film later became a cult classic.

Lance Carson was a member of the new generation of Malibu point surfers during the 1950s, along with Mickey Muñoz, Kemp Aaberg, and Mickey Dora. Lance was noted for power turns and assiduous noseriding.
John Severson collection

Harry "Skip" Frye is known as a surfer's surfer. A master of the trim, he has maintained the soulful flame of surfing since he first got wet. He's always been a purist, a guardian of the tenets of free-spirit surfing in the best tradition of Duke Kahanamoku.

Harry "Skip" Frye
The Master of Trim

Harry Frye, known simply as "Skip," is the ideal example of what a young gremmie 1960s surfer would be like if ever there was one. Skip, always in paddling shape, is medium built with reddish brown complexion, white-blond hair, and a genuine welcoming smile.

As a 16-year-old, Skip began his surfing lifestyle, and over a half a century, he proceeded to make his mark in the competition circuits, winning a multitude of trophies and accolades. In 1991, he was inducted into the Surfing Hall of Fame, and in 2000 he won the *Longboard* magazine readers' poll master's division.

Free-surfing is where you see the real personality of the surfriders surface and display their story. What surfing means to him or her and how it is translated shows in a surfer's riding style. Skip's story is like no other surfer. He "milks" the wave down to the last inch. He's a master of "the trim," sometimes appearing to glide like a soaring pelican riding the air waves above the crest.

Paul Strauch

Hawai'i's Gentleman Surfrider

Paul Strauch is Hawai'i's answer to smooth-style surfing. Always
in control, Strauch made turning his longboard look effortless.
Starting out surfing in Waikiki at four years of age, Paul went
on to develop his international competitive surfing skills over
the years with multiple wins in Hawai'i and Peru. A third-place
acknowledgement in *Surfer* magazine's Readers' Poll, 1963–1965,
underlined his peers' appreciation for his skill.

Strauch is probably most famous for developing the
"Strauch Stretch" or "Cheater Five," a move that combined
crouching and extending the front foot onto the nose of the
board, sort of a noseride move, but not quite.

Always a well versed and approachable gentleman in a sea
of aggressive competitors, Strauch maintained the manners of a
quiet Hawai'ian gentleman surfrider.

**Hawai'i's own Paul Strauch has won his share of surfing acclaim. This
time, the Duke himself was there to congratulate Paul as runner-up
in the prestigious Duke Kahanamoku Invitational.** *John Severson*

David "Dewey" Weber

Legendary Hot-dogger

Dewey Weber was the legendary hot-dogger of Malibu, California, during the 1950s. Weber was known throughout the burgeoning surf world as the "little man on wheels" due to his quick skillful steps to the nose of the longboard and back again that he would repeat several times in succession if necessary. Weber stood 5 feet 3 inches and weighed in at 130 pounds of lean, well-conditioned muscle. He additionally possessed the skills of a world-class athlete. His surfing mastery over the years earned him a lion's share of accolades and trophies. Weber was featured in most of the original surf movies of the late 1950s and early 1960s, such as *Slippery When Wet*, *Cat on a Hot Foam Board*, and *Walk on the Wet Side*, all of which permanently recorded his place in surfing's history.

During the 1960s, Dewey Weber Surfboards was a South Bay, California, high-profile powerhouse board-building company. Master shapers Harold Iggy and Donald Takayama shaped most of Dewey's extra-wide (potato chip) plan shapes that allowed for easy turning and stability, especially in the small-wave market of the East Coast. Weber developed a very cool, progressive marketing campaign that was clever, intuitive, and coupled with an endorsement from Australia's world champion, Nat Young, and the red-jacketed Weber Surf Team. Dewey Weber Surfboards excelled and was internationally renowned.

When surf historians look back on the twentieth century's outstanding surfers and the art of hot-dogging, Dewey surely will be the surfer of choice.

International Surfing magazine's Hall of Fame inducted Dewey Weber in 1966.

David "Dewey" Weber made surfboards that worked for his hot-dogging style of surfing at Malibu. They were also perfect for East Coast waves. *Tom Servais*

Robert "Nat" Young

Grand Master Surfrider

Robert Young, known internationally as "Nat," is Australia's twentieth-century surfing titan. A 6-foot-plus, lanky, muscular, chiseled Moses, with a tendency to crack a real smile, Nat presided over a level of international surfing competition that required a shark-eyed determination and confidence to be successful, so it shouldn't come as a surprise that Nat, once on dry land, might carry on with the subjects he finds nurturing. A self-taught author, Nat has successfully penned six surfing books, made two surfing documentaries, and created a 90-minute film on the history of Australian surfing. An environmentalist who puts his money and effort where his mouth is, he ran for political office and was an outspoken critic of the taint professional competition does to the ideals of surfing: "Surfing's underpinning is an art form," he said.

Nat's accomplishment in professional surfing is an acknowledged masterful achievement recognized worldwide by those aficionados who followed surfing history. As Nat matured, he began to return more toward his basic surf roots and the unique clear values of free-surfing. Along the run, Nat made the American-based *Surfer* magazine Readers' Poll in 1961. He won a place in the 1996 *International Surfing* Hall of Fame, and got a spot in the lineup in Australia's Surfing Hall of Fame. Finally, he received his plaque on the Surfing Walk of Fame in 1996 at Huntington Beach, cementing his grand master surfrider legacy.

Robert "Nat" Young won the 1966 surfing world title in San Diego and was so far ahead, he announced that he'd be willing to start over again if they wanted to make the contest more interesting. After years of participating in international surfriding contests and gaining peer respect for his surfing innovations, Nat returned to his philosophical support of the basic tenets of freestyle free-spirit surfing.

Bob McTavish
Australian Master Board Designer and Surfer

In 1992, the Aussie Bob McTavish was anointed by *Surfing Life* magazine as the most influential shaper of all time. Later, in 1996, McTavish was inducted into Australia's Surfing Hall of Fame. As a preteen, McTavish took up surfing when he was 12 and then, finding it to his liking, kept on going to become one of Australia's legendary surfriders and internationally acclaimed shapers. His creative innovation, the "V-bottom" shortboard in 1967, made him a shaping legend. Coming from the Aussie's perspective, the "flow with it era" of California did not allow for all that could be achieved on a wave.

The shortboard made that argument best, besides, being involved was fun. So Bob, shortboard and V-bottom in hand, looked to "using the power of the wave to maneuver really fast without loss of speed," much like George Greenough, only standing up. Clearly, to McTavish, the boards had to be lighter and shorter than the flavor of the time, the 9-foot, 6-inch heavyweights, which flat out couldn't be maneuvered in that helter-skelter style.

Surfing contests eventually lost their appeal to McTavish after he won the Queensland's State Championship consecutively from 1964 to 1966, when he also took third place in the Aussie nationals.

McTavish dropped out of surfing in the 1970s and came back for one more swing, touting the benefits of longboarding and the longboard itself as another way to have fun surfing.

In 1989, creative board builder Bob McTavish introduced machine-molded replicas of the top surfriders' signature surfboards, a concept way ahead of its commercial acceptance.
John Witzig

Dick Catri
Godfather of East Coast Surfing

Dick Catri is a multitasker surfer from Florida who has had the kind of positive influence on East Coast surfing's growth that has earned him the handle of the godfather of East Coast surfing. As the East was just beginning to get its sea legs, Dick was learning his surfing craft on Hawai'i's North Shore, doing gremmie work at first—sweeping up, fixing dings, learning to shape, glassing boards, multitasking. In between working for food, Dick was the first East Coast surfer to ride the Banzai Pipeline and take on big Waimea Bay.

Returning to Florida, Dick opened up his Satellite Beach Surf Shop, created a powerful East Coast surf team, and ran a streak of wins that included toppling Dewey Weber, "the little man on wheels," that gave back to East Coast surfers the stature they lost when Mickey Dora dubbed the East Coast surf, "dishwater waves." Following this event, Dick was invited to the prestigious Duke Kahanamoku Invitational.

If that was not enough, Dick founded the Florida Pro world tour contest in the 1970s, continued to surf in the Senior Division of the U.S. Championships, and later coached Kelly Slater when he was a teenager. Dick also started the annual Easter Surfing Festival in Cocoa Beach Florida, and was inducted into both the International Surfing Hall of Fame and the East Coast Surfing Hall of Fame.

Before settling down in Melbourne Beach, Florida, Dick Catri surfaried to Hawai'i and spent his formative surfing years exploring and riding the big surf of the North Shore. *Dick Graham*

"Everything changed; it was the beginning of no longer looking at the East Coast like you're all a bunch of kooks."

—*Dick Catri*

Wayne Lynch was the Australian acclaimed master of the shortboard while still in his teens.

Wayne Lynch

Innovator of the Shortboard Revolution

In 1999, *Surfer* magazine picked Wayne Lynch as the thirteenth most influential surfer of all time. This acknowledgement came thirty-six years after Lynch made his debut in Australian's open age state contest and by all accounts won the thing. Alas, the judges felt he was too young, so they agreed to give him the "wave of the day" award instead of the first-place trophy. Wayne was 11 years old, and about to usher in the shortboard era all by himself. Two years later, he entered the juniors division of the Victoria state titles and took home six consecutive titles.

Wayne was by all Australian accounts their teenage wonder boy. Over time, he proved them right with Paul Witzig's 1969 core film *Evolution*, where Wayne introduced the shortboard's unlimited possibilities and his ability to get upside down in the curl. The future had been discovered, and now the new wave of progressive surfriders were free to go anywhere, anytime. Everything was possible.

As with a lot of extraordinary surfers, the rise to fame can be daunting. Surfing by its very nature is sincerely personal, so to be suddenly thrown upon a world stage is conflicting—especially if it's not in your nature or desire to be singled out and heralded. As Wayne said, he "wasn't interested in fame" or money; he wanted to be "just a surfer, not a star." So there lies his emotional conflict, which has always been at odds with Wayne's need for a quiet lifestyle with the opportunity to surf alone, and yet to still be an exemplary athletic surfer who's talent automatically draws admiration from novices and aficionados alike.

In 1988, Wayne Lynch was brought into Australia's Surfing Hall of Fame.

George Greenough
Visionary, Vanguard, Innovator, and Surfer

George Greenough is acclaimed throughout the surfing hierarchy as one of twentieth-century surfing's most influential surfers, shapers, and photographers. As a kneeboard surfer, a decision he made to get closer to the wave's surface, Greenough, riding his specialized board, opened the path to the eventual shortboard revolution by ripping full-speed bank turns that simply could not be achieved with the awkward heavyweight longboards. His 4-foot-plus creatively designed, flexible spoon kneeboard with a fiberglass kneeling area and foam edges allowed for radical, deep, cutbacks never before imagined. Bob McTavish, watching Greenough's sweeping maneuvers, was so impressed that he designed his own V-bottom shortboard to allow standing surfers to emulate the same maneuverability as Greenough on his kneeboard.

Greenough's surf film, *The Innermost Limits of Pure Fun*, was filmed with a 28-pound waterproof camera that he mounted on his shoulder. The film exposed for the first time to the surfing world the inside workings of tubing waves. Greenough was able to get so far back in the tube that the core surfing audience, awestruck, would holler and hoot throughout the entire movie. With George's exploratory film, the surfing barriers that once were imposing or simply not yet conceived were forever torn down, and the fresh possibilities in store for surfing at once became evident.

Australia's world champion, Nat Young, was quoted in 1968 as saying that George Greenough was the "greatest surfer in the world today."

George Greenough is probably a genius; his contributions to surfing innovation certainly point to that conclusion. *Greg Huglin*

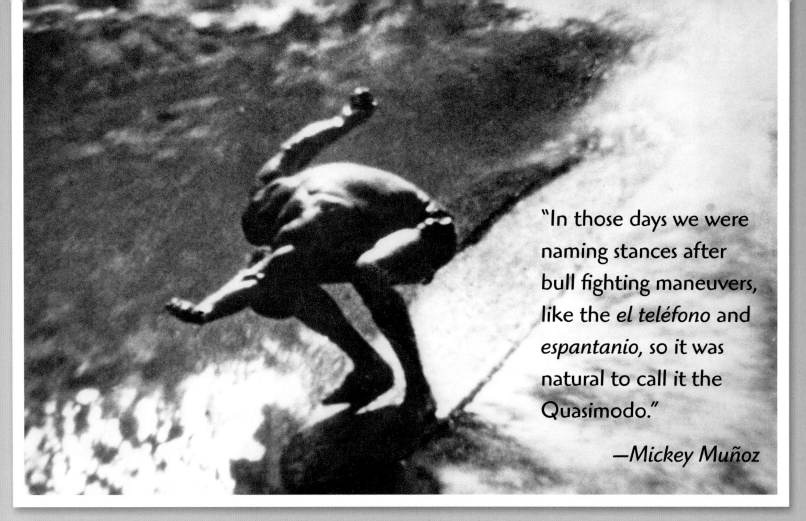

"In those days we were naming stances after bull fighting maneuvers, like the *el teléfono* and *espantanio*, so it was natural to call it the Quasimodo."

—Mickey Muñoz

Mickey Muñoz is a surfer's surfer who has devoted his life to chasing waves anytime, anywhere. *John Severson*

Mickey Muñoz
A Surfer's Surfer

Mickey Muñoz was born an enthusiastic surfer in New York City and quickly made his way to Santa Monica where he began his surfing career at the age of 10. It wasn't long before Muñoz stood out as one of the hot riders of the Malibu Pit in the 1950s.

Mickey was an adventuresome waterman from the moment he first got wet. He loved the ocean, and it was recognized early on that he was not only a big-wave chaser (he was a part of the original crew to ride Waimea Bay in 1957), but he could master small waves, too. To that end, Muñoz was featured in John Severson's first issue of *Surfer* magazine doing Mexican bullfighting moves, "*el teléfono*," and what would become his iconic crouch, "the Quasimodo," named after Victor Hugo's Hunchback of Notre Dame. It was all done in fun, and it stuck with Muñoz for the rest of his surfing career, even though he never repeated the moves again until 2008 when he was filmed doing them once more just for fun.

As a competitor, Mickey held his own in the contest scene of the 1950s and 1960s, taking second place in the 1962 and 1963 West Coast Championships. In 1964, he placed third in the United States championships. Muñoz' best competitive year was 1965. He placed second in the United States championships, fourth in the world championships, and was an inaugural invitee to the notable and exclusive Duke Kahanamoku Invitational. Muñoz arguably won the 1965 Tom Morey noseriding contest, too, although that is still in dispute more than four decades later. Called "the Mongoose," Muñoz was an outstanding competitor, and his love of surfing goes even further. If ever there was an example of what it's like to live the surfer lifestyle, Muñoz is that surfer. He's devoted his life to the Sport of Kings and every aficionado would agree that "the Goose" is one of them! Mickey is truly a surfer's surfer.

Robert August
Endless Summer *Surfrider*

Robert August, a hard-core goofy-footer from Seal Beach, California, came from the old-school tradition of surfing, which in essence translated into functional, stylish maneuvers that flowed with the wave. He is the perfect example of the "good surfer." August's reputation of having a classic, smooth, deliberate style of riding a wave earned him a coveted co-starring spot in Bruce Brown's search for the perfect wave, *Endless Summer*. The 1966 surf film documented the turning point of surfing's acceptance as a noble endeavor and was an internationally acclaimed hit. Fortunately for August, he was swept along on that perfect endless wave and was able to ride with it for half a century, enjoying the fame while keeping his roots in his love of surfing.

In 2001, August's home town of Huntington Beach inducted him into its Surfing Walk of Fame, adding one more honor to his collection.

When you think about it, Robert August has lived the endless-summer lifestyle, chasing that perfect wave. It will always remain a rewarding way to spend a lifetime. *Bruce Brown*

The vanguard noserider of his era was simply called "David," and when you used that first name, everyone knew exactly who you were talking about—David Nuuhiwa. He was that famous and that good, especially when crouching through small California surf or perched on the nose for 10 seconds at a time. *Leo Hetzel*

David Nuuhiwa

Master of the Nose

David Nuuhiwa was magical on the nose. He had a style that was very smooth and very cool. Aficionados of surfing acknowledge that Nuuhiwa ruled the nose. Beyond that, he was a proficient surfer in all aspects of small-wave riding. His ability to master the waves was uncanny and would cause those watching to drop their jaws and hoot, "Far-out!"

David was born in Hawai'i in 1948 and began his surfing career at the age of 5. His father was a beach boy and also a grand master of the martial arts. When he was 13, Nuuhiwa moved to California and eventually took shelter in 1962 with Donald Takayama and Harold Iggy, premier board builders for Dewey Weber. From 1964 through 1966, Nuuhiwa took the lead in the United States Surfing Association circuit, showing that he was the man, a unique surfer, light years ahead of his contemporaries. Nuuhiwa continued his run at the contest scene for more than a decade, but even as a teenager, he was considered to be one of the world's best surfers.

Nuuhiwa won the U.S. championship in 1968 and 1971. In 1972, he was the spectator favorite to win the World Contest, and it looked like he had won it over Jimmy Blears in the finals. He got second.

In 1966 and 1967, he was chosen as the World's Best Surfer by *International Surfing* magazine. In 1991, David was inducted by the International Surfing Hall of Fame; then he received his honor on the Huntington Beach Surfing Walk of Fame.

Herbie Fletcher

Master Longboard Waterman

Herbie Fletcher has always thought outside the box. It's his nature. He's always doing far-out things before anyone else even thinks about it, like his Astrodeck traction pads (gripping adhesive), the early production of hard-core surf videos featuring longboard adventures, and the single-handed instigating of the return to prominence of the longboard surfriding resurgence with the slogan "the thrill is back." It came back and stayed.

To his credit, probably the most far-reaching idea Herbie dreamed up was the towing in of surfers to ride the 25-foot Waimea Bay and 12-foot Pipeline. Fletcher was the forerunner of the eventual assault on Jaws, Maui.

Fletcher's surfriding skills also need acknowledgement. In 1966, he was in the semifinals of the World Contest in San Diego, and he won the juniors division of the Laguna Masters in the same year, then came in second in the United States Surfing Association juniors division ratings.

Herbie made the cover of *Surfer* magazine, hanging ten on his longboard in 1995, when *Surfer* had gone to exclusively featuring shortboards. That was far out!

Huntington Beach inducted Herbie Fletcher into its Surfing Walk of Fame in 1995.

Herbie Fletcher is one of those surfriders who always seem to be having more fun while pushing the envelope on the unknown. It ain't bragging if you can do it, and everybody knows Herbie don't brag.

Christian Fletcher

Aerial Rebel

Christian Fletcher took the aerials of the 1970s and fine-tuned them in the 1980s so that flying above the crest line became an integral part of modern surfing.

Christian Fletcher loved to fly. He liked getting air. It was his calling. Although Fletcher didn't invent the aerial, he did give it credence. Aerials are fun, a lot of fun. Aficionados can debate forever if aerials have any true function, and that question is always raised when something new is being brought to the party. Yet, the art of aerials is here to stay, thanks mostly to Christian's inventive and skillful demonstrations above the crest line.

The contest scene didn't really appeal to Fletcher, although he could do well in that arena when he tried. In 1989, the Body Glove Surfbout awarded him $31,725 for trying and winning their event. It was a record cash prize, but it didn't endear Christian to competition; he was all about free-surfing, having fun, and getting above it all.

Jackie and Josh Baxter
The Family That Surfs Together

You could always count on Jackie Baxter to surprise you when you were watching him surf. When he *should* have dropped quickly to the bottom of the wave for the centrifugal force to propel him back up to the lip, he'd make a quick snap turn midway down the wave, tempting the pitching curl before completing the drop to the trough, then, almost as an afterthought, complete the force turn. Baxter, of course, would usually make the wave by the narrowest of margins—*usually* being the operative word. It was his unexpected moves that earned him his reputation for being spontaneous and how he made his mark on the North Shore's "good surfer" list.

Jackie Baxter's family, from their beginning, lived the lifestyle of a surf family with roots dug deep into the surfing philosophy. Josh Baxter, Jackie's son, was born on the North Shore of Oahu and has carried on the Baxter family tradition by surfing all of his life all over the world, opening a surfing school and winning the United States Longboard Championships three times.

The family that surfs together rides the carefree lifestyle together.

"The drop" for some surfers is the best part of riding the wave—and the most artistic. Here's Jackie Baxter at work.

"Through the longboard tour and meshing of personalities, I was fortunate to learn the ways and waves of the west side through the Aloha of the locals like Rusty K, Lance, and the rest of crew including Bonga, Dino and Joey. Personally and professionally this photo represents a peak period of my life with the ending of the 1994 longboard tour in Hawai'i, and being crowned U.S. tour champ at Makaha. To use this shot on the cover of a magazine with a focus on Hawai'i and soul surfing adds deeply to the meaning of this photo.

"So this photo represents acceptance; and accomplishment of hard work and returning the Aloha. And using that acceptance for pushing my surfing, otherwise it can be hard to imagine a cover shot with a dry-haired blonde haole, way up on the nose of a yellow/red longboard without a leash on the pre-bowl section of a crisp one at Makaha. It may happen, but not often. The point is that it reflects on the goodness of the community at Makaha, for which I will always be grateful. It is one of the most core and genuine surf areas on this planet; and I thank them for their role in my surfing life, and scoring this cover shot!"

—Josh Baxter

"Commitment, control and confidence. That is what this photo means to me. While I have the pride of a son, any real surfer who looks at this photo can easily see the high degree of commitment.

"But for me, I see commitment on various dimensions. I see his obvious commitment to this jacking wave at Pipeline; but I also see his commitment to a pure surfing lifestyle. I see his commitment to the Hawai'ian Islands, and symbolically, I see his commitment to balance his life with family, surf, and Aloha.

"When I travel the world and people say 'he's Jackie Baxter's son,' photos like this explain how and why he earned his respect and reputation.

"With the back foot centered over the stringer, left foot and heel on the inside rail, and hands positioned for a controlled vertical drop, the image of his stance even without the wave has become an iconic symbol for our family.

"But it is also imprinted into me mentally, and onto me physically. For the love of surfing and the path my dad has laid out, this photo is ground-zero as far as binding me with my dad; and inspiring my own version of commitment to surf and live with balance and stoke."

—Josh Baxter

Josh Baxter rides the nose at Makaha Beach. *Jim Russi*

Although no one could define what style was, you knew it when you saw it. Billy Hamilton was a 1960s proponent of "style" in the days when it still mattered, even when taking it up into the big-wave category. "Stylin'" in trim and really moving, Billy flies through a perfect backlit sunset wave. Sometimes it can't get any better.

Bill Hamilton
The Stylist

Bill Hamilton has earned a loyal following within the surf aficionado community. They say he's a master stylist in the same realm as Phil Edwards. Always smooth and always functional, with hand movements that conducted his classic ballet turns, Hamilton represented a time during the 1960s when style still mattered.

Billy started out in California, where he developed his unique stylistic surfing method and then surfaried to Hawai'i when he began his assault on the Islands' power wave. He was able to maintain his signature style even as he rode waves that were much bigger and more challenging.

While living in the Islands, Hamilton began moving away slowly from the contest scene, taking part in the Duke Kahanamoku Invitational and Pipeline Masters, before completely moving on to free-surfing.

Billy lives on Kauai and continues to surf and shape boards, which is the surfer's way of living the good life.

Mark Martinson punctuated his surfing career by winning the 1965 U.S. championship on a longboard before making the transition to shortboards in the 1970s. *Leo Hetzel*

Mark Martinson
Master Surfrider

Mark Martinson, a friendly, good-natured surfer from Long Beach, California, was born in 1947. He began surfing at the age of 10 and placed in the 1962 West Coast Championships, then two years later he took first place in the United States Invitational. Martinson, a regular-foot power surfer, completed his competitive career in 1965 by winning the men's division of the United States Surfing Championships.

MacGillivray and Freeman, the core surf film team of the late 1960s, featured Martinson in their groundbreaking surf film, *Free and Easy* in 1967, which included global surf travel to Peru, Brazil, Argentina, France, Spain, Portugal, and Hawai'i. In 1970, Martinson was featured once again in another M&F surf film, *Waves of Change*. It was by all measures a lucky break and a dream come true for a surfer to travel to those remote places and get to surf at uncrowded surf spots, while becoming a surf movie star. It was a four-year, all-expenses-paid world tour: Yee Ha!

Martinson eventually moved to Hawai'i and settled on the North Shore of Oahu, where he adapted to shortboard surfing and board building before releasing his Mark Martinson Model through Robert August Surfboards of California.

Felipe Pomar
Peruvian World Champion

Felipe Pomar is proof, if ever it was needed, that surfers come from all walks of life. Felipe, an aristocratic Peruvian surfrider, was his country's national sports treasure, winning three Peruvian international titles and running up in two more. In 1965, he won the World Surfing Championship at Punta Rocas to become the first Latin American international surfing champion. Hawai'i called in 1963, so Felipe surfaried to the Hawai'ian Islands and participated in the Duke Kahanamoku Invitational four times.

This is hard to believe, yet it's true: Felipe Pomar rode a tsunami, just off the west shore of Lima, Peru. Except for the oil painting in Hawai'i's Bishop Museum of a local farmer rumored to have caught a tsunami, it has never been done before or since.

In 1966 and again in 1967, *International Surfing* magazine's readers pointed to Felipe Pomar as Peru's top surfer and honorary Hall of Fame member.

Felipe Pomar was Peru's prototype big-wave champion from 1962 through 1967. He achieved a well-deserved legacy that will stand proud in the Peru Sports Hall of Fame. *Dick Graham*

Barry Kanaiaupuni

Sunset's Power Surfer

Barry Kanaiaupuni's surfing style in his era was anything but careful, wild maybe. A better description might be wild with a variety of spontaneous power maneuvers that took place at any time and any place on the wave, much to the surprise of anyone watching.

Kanaiaupuni, or B. K., was born in 1945 at the end of World War II and the reawakening of surfing at Waikiki Beach. When he was eight, B. K. started surfing. Then in 1963, Bud Brown, the master pioneer surf movie icon, discovered the teenager and slipped him into his new core film, *Gun Ho!*. That was B. K.'s start toward a long lifestyle career in what was then a neophyte surfing industry. Over the next half century, B. K. participated in enough contests to test his mettle, including all the Duke Kahanamoku Invitationals, Hang Ten Pros, and Expression Sessions. Yet, contest surfing wasn't really Kanaiaupuni's game; he was basically a go-for-it ballistic free-style surfrider with a tendency to stretch his luck, which is sure death in contest surfing.

Barry began his shaping career in 1967, starting with Rick Surfboards in Manhattan Beach, California, where he had his own signature model, then to Lightning Bolt Hawai'i, Chuck Dent in Huntington Beach, eventually opening his own series of shops on the North and West Shores of Oahu.

Barry Kanaiaupuni was a good competitor, taking part in all the Duke Kahanamoku Invitationals. Yet it wasn't really his thing. When the longboards went short, Barry came into his own. The shortboard set him free to ride as radically as he wanted.

Dane Kealoha surprised everyone except himself when, in 1977, he snuck into the finals of the world-acclaimed Duke Kahanamoku Classic at Sunset Beach, Oahu, and picked up the third-place Academy Award look-alike trophy.

Dane Kealoha

Hawai'ian Pioneer Tuberider

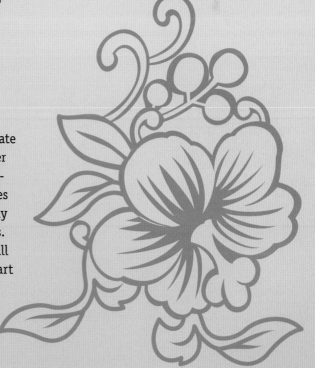

Hawai'ian Dane Kealoha started surfing successfully at the age of 14, which is late for a pro-surfer-to-be. Yet from the start, Kealoha was a gifted athlete who after surfing for a meager two years, won the boy's division of Hawai'i's state championships and three years later took the 1976 junior's division of the United States championships. The next year, Kealoha swept in and took the third-place trophy in the Duke Kahanamoku Invitational, favorably shocking the local aficionados.

Kealoha was eventually ranked number two in the surfing world, and he will be remembered as the Hawai'ian Islands' pioneer surfrider who dominated the art of tuberiding during the 1980s with his patented crouching "pig-dog" style.

Claude "Claudie" Codgen

Vaunted East Coast Waterman

Claude "Claudie" Codgen's surfing fame was stunted by the out-of-sight, out-of-mind East Coast geography handicap. When surfing started to take hold, the surf magazines looked mainly to Hawai'i for big winter wave issues and to California for summer swells coverage, with sporadic Australia-oriented articles. The East Coast, because of its small-wave reputation, was hard pressed to get any coverage at all. Sadly for Claudie, his skills were overlooked nationally, much like a major league player in small market.

Claudie won the East's junior division title in 1966, then again in 1967, and later in 1969, he won the men's division. His smooth style of surfing had been compared to Bill Hamilton's and David Nuuhiwa's, both of whom are master surfers of midsize waves from the West Coast.

Claudie began his surfing as a 12-year-old at his home breaks in the area of Florida's Cape Canaveral and Cocoa Beach. He was considered by East Coast surf aficionados as the best East Coast surfer during the mid-1960s. In 1970, he started his surfboard company, Sunshine Surfboards, shaping and running it out of Melbourne Beach, Florida.

In 1996, Claude Codgen was inducted into the inaugural East Coast Surfing Legends Hall of Fame.

Claude "Claudie" Codgen was a beautiful stylist out of Cocoa Beach, Florida. He earned a reputation for being an outstanding surfer during the late 1960s. *Dick Graham*

"I started Sunshine Surfboards in 1970. That's when the East Coast started coming of age and people were demanding good boards made for the type of surf we have here, but they're generally just a little wider, a little flatter bottom, and can move on top of the water as opposed to sinking down in it, like Hawai'i or a bigger wave."

—*Claude Codgen*

Gary Propper was a master small-wave East Coast surfer, and his win over Dewey Weber in the East Coast Championship elevated his ranking to international caliber. *Ron Stoner*

Mike Tabeling
East Coast International Surfrider

Mike Tabeling was an amateur surfrider who surfed like a pro from the beginning. Surfing very tall with swooping winglike arms, Tabeling, a 6-foot, 4-inch surfer from Cocoa Beach, Florida, would come into his own during the mid-1960s with multiple wins in the East Coast Junior Championships. When Tabeling took first place in the junior division of the West Coast Laguna Masters, the win laid down the marker that East Coast surfers could compete and win in national competitions. In 1968, Tabeling took second place in the men's division of the United States championships at Huntington Beach, California, behind world-renowned noserider champion, David Nuuhiwa. With that accomplishment, Tabeling became the first recognized East Coast international surfer after big-wave pioneer rider Dick Catri.

Completing an extensive surfari in Africa, Australia, and Europe, Tabeling returned to the United States in 1996, just in time to be inducted into the original East Coast Surfing Legends Hall of Fame.

Mike Tabeling laid down the Eastern surfriders' marker when he went west and demonstrated that the East Coast surfers were "contenders."

Gary Propper
East Coast Premier Hot-dogger

Gary Propper will always be known as the skilled young hot-dogger from Cocoa Beach, Florida, who took on and won against the "little man on wheels," Dewey Weber, during the 1966 East Coast Final. For an East Coast surfer to beat Dewey Weber in a surfing event forever changed the attitude the East had about itself. Now they could hold their heads high. No longer would their surf be compared with the "dishwater waves" that Mickey Dora scoffed at. Now they had their pride, and they could compete with the West and win. Game on!

Propper carried his confidence and contest surfing aggression into his business career, teaming up with Hobie Surfboards to make his signature Gary Propper model. He scored big! In 1967, his model sold more than 3,000 boards, more than any other signature model at that time. Never one not to maximize his opportunities, Propper also repped for Kanvas by Katin and O'Neill Wetsuits. The combination made Propper the number one professional surfer of his era.

International Surfing magazine awarded Propper a slot in its Hall of Fame in 1967, and in 1996 the inaugural East Coast Surfing Legends Hall of Fame inducted him into its fellowship.

PART 3

The PROGRESSIVE SURFRIDERS

THE PIONEERING STAGE OF THE surfing evolution started around the beginning of the twentieth century with the father of surfing, Duke Kahanamoku, leading the way. Things changed during the 1960s. Surfers still continued to pioneer and explore the world, looking for exotic surf spots, but their surfboards went into the surf shops for an overhaul. The major improvements to the pivotal surfboard were the creation of foam and going short.

When the 1970s arrived, the next progressive generation of surfriders were ready to go with state-of-the-art equipment. No longer dominated and handicapped by the size and weight of the surfboard; the philosophy of surfing was also freed up. Now instead of having to flow with it, with cool stylistic maneuvers, the doors were flown open to skate the surf, to explore the wave itself, to rip it, to tear it, to lacerate it, to go where no surfer had gone before.

For the last three decades of the twentieth century, the level of surfing by the new wave of progressive surfrider exploded. One only has to look at what has been accomplished. The progressive surfriders have opened "back doors," blatantly dominated the Pipeline, and have the audacity to run contests at Waimea Bay, Jaws, and Todo Santos, while continuing to search the seven seas for ever larger monster waves to conquer.

It's safe to say that the story of the last few decades of twentieth century surfing were overwhelmingly dominated by the athletic prowess of the finely tuned progressive surfrider and his and her equipment.

Shaun Tomson
Legendary South African Surfrider

When Shaun Tomson first surfed onto the professional surfing stage, he brought with him a well-mannered, eloquent gentleman's perspective. Born in 1955 in Durban, South Africa, Tomson took up the sport of surfing at age 10. Within two years, Shaun won the boys division of the South African National Championships. That set up his course, and from there his professional surfing achievements unfurled like a spinnaker catching wind.

Early on in the 1970s, Shaun won the South African Durban Gunston 500 six (count them) times in a row, and in 1975 he won the Hang Ten Pro in Hawai'i. Next he went back-side, winning one of the most treacherous Banzai Pipeline contests ever in gnarly 10- to 12-foot surf. When Tomson decided to hang it up after an enviable amateur and professional surfing career culminating in 1989, he had won 12 world tour contests over two decades. He was world champion in 1978.

Tomson's most notable surfing legacy will be his unprecedented domination of the tube, like those at Backdoors. With weaving movements to and fro within the barrel, Tomson was able to climb, drop, and drop again, gaining speed from deeper and deeper inside the curl. His pioneering moves are still used by those surfers who like to disappear from view.

In 1978, the readers' poll of *Surfer* magazine awarded Tomson their "Outstanding Surfer of the Year" vote. The South African Sports Hall of Fame adopted him in that same year, the Jewish Hall of Fame acknowledged him, and the Huntington Beach Surfing Walk of Fame bestowed a tribute that bears his name. Thomson was named by Australia's *Surfing Life* magazine as "surfing's all-time best tube rider."

Climbing backdoors and drop-tuberiding will probably be Shaun Tomson's legacy—as well as winning the 1977 World Championship.

With an unorthodox and unique style, labeled the Wounded Gull, Mark Richards was able to win four consecutive world championships.

Mark Richards
The Wounded Gull

Mark Richards, Australia's "wounded gull" surfrider, would take his 6-foot, 1-inch, 170-pound body and twist and contort it into a radical torque, tearing and lacerating, wave-stomping, human missile. By doing so, he dominated his era's professional surfing men's division by winning, just for example, four consecutive world championships from 1979 through 1982, the Smirnoff Waimea Bay Pro Am, and the World Cup at Sunset Beach.

After many years of shaping his own boards, and with an insightful influence from master shapers Dick Brewer and Reno Abellira, Mark fine-tuned his famous twin-fin short-board that gave him the edge he needed for radical moves on waves of all sizes, especially the smaller ones usually found during surf contests.

Richards was awarded the *Surfer* magazine readers' poll three times, *Surfer*'s "Surfer of the Year" award three times, and he was invited into the first Australian Surfing Hall of Fame in 1985. America's Huntington Beach, California, Surfing Walk of Fame inducted him in 1994.

His home country honored Richards in 1994 with the Order of Australia Medal.

Wayne "Rabbit" Bartholomew
Australian Legendary Champion

Wayne Bartholomew, a.k.a. "Rabbit," because he was fast, won the 1978 World Championship because he earned it through perseverance, wave knowledge, tactics, and a lot of practice. Wayne is the classic example of a great athlete—a champion who improves upon his natural skills by studying all aspects of the sport. Bartholomew did all this with sincerity and diligence, involving himself in professional surfing associations, surf environmentalism, authoring books and surf columns, coaching amateur and professional surfers alike, and becoming president and executive director of the Association of Surfing Professionals (ASP).

Although Bartholomew won eight world tour contests, finished three times in the finals of the Pipeline Masters, and more, what made these accomplishments special was his vivacious and playful lifestyle. He loved surfing and he loved to show off—a fun combination. Like an actor with a sense of humor, Rabbit brought more than his skills to surfing.

Australia's Hall of Fame honored Wayne Bartholomew in 1987, and Huntington Beach's Surfing Walk of Fame inducted him in 2001.

Wayne "Rabbit" Bartholomew was a serious student of the sport of surfing as well as a devoted organizer of the Association of Surfing Professionals. As a professional surfer, Rabbit won the Big One—the world championship of 1978.

Peter Townend
Master Australian Stylist

When it comes to surfing with a sense of "styling,"
Australian-born surfer Peter Townend, a.k.a. "P. T.,"
is the classic example of the appreciated skill. P. T.'s
extended soul-arch bottom turns are likened to
the beautiful posing arches of the Hawai'ian beach
boy surfers of Waikiki from the 1930s to the 1950s.
P. T.'s stylish skills also lead to comparisons with the
matador and bull—the wave and the surfer, function
and style.

In the aggressive game of competitive surfing,
P. T. scooped up more than his share of both amateur
and professional awards, and trophies from 1965
through 1977, including a world title and an enviable
second place in the prestigious Duke Kahanamoku
Invitational at Sunset Beach, Oahu. In 1978, P. T.
decided to go back to free surfing, putting aside his
professional surfing career. Wanting to keep close
to his surf roots, P. T. took up working within the
California surf culture, specializing in executive
directing of surf team organizations. Because of
his surfing knowledge and his professional media
skills, he soon became the go-to spokesman, master
of ceremonies, and contest announcer for most of
California's surf events.

Townend's recognized capabilities in his support-
ive roles are based upon his insight and experience in
international surfing. Of course, being a 1976 world
champion underlines his credentials. Add to that his
Aussie accent, and that seals the deal.

In addition to being a multifaceted surf culture contributor,
Peter Townend is a remarkably stylish surfer whose radical
moves—including beautiful cutbacks and soul arches—have
changed the future of modern surfing. Peter was not limited
to beautiful soul arches. He had in his quiver a number of
aggressive maneuvers as illustrated by this cutback using
his arm as a pivot to turn—the classic progressive surfer.

Terry Fitzgerald
The Sultan of Speed

Nobody knew if Terry Fitzgerald was really going faster than anyone else, but he sure looked like it. Surfing like a man being chased, styling, and hair flying in the wind, "Fitz" was known as the "sultan of speed." Of course, like most Aussie surfriding champions, Fitz was also a "take no prisoners competitor" as a rookie, and he began chasing surf trophies early in his competitive career. He made his first move by jumping on and driving the revolutionary shortboard to the semi-finals in the 1970 World Surfing Championships held in Victoria, Australia. Fitz then started his competitive surf lifestyle run by picking up wins at the 1972 Bell's Beach, Australia, contest, the 1975 Lightning Bolt contest held at Velzyland on Oahu, and eventually he became the Australian national champion in 1975. On the surf culture front, Fitzgerald played his part by co-founding the Australian Professional Surfing Association and Hot Buttered, his surfboard company, sponsored the Pro Junior contest, an international review of the next generation of hot young grommets.

Terry Fitzgerald, the sultan of speed, was welcomed into Australia's Surfing Hall of Fame in 1995.

No, it wasn't an illusion of speed, although it may have looked that way at first glance. The speed was real, and Terry Fitzgerald was going as fast as he appeared to be going here at Sunset Beach on Oahu, Hawai'i. He was, after all, the sultan of speed.

Peter Drouyn
Australia's Legendary Stylist

Peter Drouyn left his mark on professional surfing in the 1970s by creating the "man-on-man" contest format, much like the one adopted in professional skiing. The format was a success and is being used to this day.

Drouyn, a regular-foot surfer from Surfers' Paradise Queensland, Australia, was born in 1949. Nine years later, he entered the surf and began a long career of amateur and professional surf competition, including international participation in the 1974 Smirnoff, the Duke Kahanamoku Invitational, and the world championship. Drouyn's claim to fame most probably lies in his winning the 1970 Australian National Titles and a sixth place ranking in the world in 1977.

Underneath all of Drouyn's accomplishments in the professional surfing world lies a creative innovative young man who consistently thought outside the box and surfed there, too. He was first and foremost an outstanding stylist complete with power and control.

Peter Drouyn brought drama to surfing, lighting it up with classic stylistic surf maneuvers and innovative contest concepts with formats that are still relevant.

Montgomery "Buttons" Kaluhiokalani held court during the 1970s shortboard emergence. He surfed with a combination of wild extravagance and complete control. Buttons was Hawai'i's answer to the new generation of shortboard hot-doggers.

Montgomery "Buttons" Kaluhiokalani
Hot Hawai'ian Surfrider

Montgomery Kaluhiokalani, a.k.a. "Buttons," set the Hawai'ian hot-dog standard for surfing during the wild, free-style 1970s, when attacking the wave was the mindset of the new breed of radical surfers.

Beginning in 1973, Buttons' surfriding skills were akin to being erratic with a purpose. He slipped into new rooms on the wave, never leaving any of them alone for long, sometimes returning quickly, and always, from a different angle. During the 1970s, Buttons was the man, the surfriding athlete with unparalleled natural ability. He could blow everybody away when he wanted to, go crazy, and yet still be able to seriously concentrate when he wanted to, which allowed him to win when he wanted to.

Buttons gathered in his share of titles and trophies throughout his surfing career, and yet he always remained a wild, happy, and free-spirited Hawai'ian surfer at heart. That reputation got him into the surf films of the time and a spot on NBC's *Real People*. Later, a cover shot on *Surfing* magazine sealed his fame as one of the "Twenty Who Rip."

Mark Occhilupo
Pro Surfer Archetype

Australian Mark Occhilupo was the archetype of professional contest surfers. Born in 1966, Occhilupo started surfing at the age of 9. By 1983, he had quit school and committed to surfing's world pro circuit and was rated 16th at the age of 17. That was the start of a radical professional lifestyle that went from the top to the bottom of the tour's competitive ranking throughout his tenure.

Nicknamed the "Raging Bull," Occhilupo was a physically strong surfer who depended mostly on his ability to finesse the midsize waves he preferred.

Occhilupo was highly regarded in the pro surf world as a superior surfer in a class by himself, but with friendliness and a tendency to be emotional. He appeared in several surf movies throughout his career, including the widely distributed Hollywood film, *North Shore*, where he was featured as himself. Over the decades, Occhilupo was an astute contestant, and he won the 1999 World Professional Title at the age of 33. He eventually racked up a total of 12 world tour event victories.

In 2000, Mark Occhilupo was given a star on the Huntington Beach Surfing Walk of Fame.

Everybody loves to see someone beat the odds, beat the buzzer, make a comeback. Mark Occhilupo did so by winning the 1999 World Championship with pure, unadulterated resolve.

Michael Peterson
Australian Power Surfrider

In 1985, *Surfer* magazine pointed to Australia's Michael Peterson as one of "25 Surfers Whose Surfing Changed the Sport." Michael was tall and powerful with an attitude of abandonment, and his outstanding athletic skills set him apart from his contemporaries. Peterson honed his skills in midrange surf, yet he wasn't limited to that size. In the 1970s, Michael was able to leave multiple contest tracks in Australia, winning among many achievements the famous Queensland and Bell's Beach titles.

Deliberate and soul searching, perhaps bashful, Michael got the call in 1992 from Australia's Surfing Hall of Fame, and *Surfer* magazine reached out again naming Michael Peterson as one of the most influential surfers of the twentieth century.

This photo of Michael Peterson is a classic illustration of the influence the shortboard had on the evolution of surfing.

Larry Bertlemann took hot-dog surfing to a new dimension of radical skate/surf moves that signaled real change in the way the next generation of young gremmies would approach surfing medium-size waves. Here's the "Rubber Man" at Ala Moana, Honolulu, Hawai'i.

Larry Bertlemann
"Rubber Man"

Larry Bertlemann, the 1973 United States surfing champion, was known as the "Rubber Man" because of the extreme, radical moves he employed in his surfing-skateboarding style. An exceptionally skilled surfer who led the way with aerials in the 1970s, he was also an equally accomplished skateboarder. Bertlemann neatly combined the two to bring a totally fresh approach to maneuvering on a wave. The extreme turns that were put together smoothly eventually took him to fourth place in the 1972 world championships, first place in the 1973 Hawai'ian state championship, first in the 1974 Duke Kahanamoku Invitational, and second in the 1975 Lightning Bolt Pro. Bertlemann's success was wide and varied and came with a supporting cast of commercial business agreements and strong corporate sponsors.

Bertlemann's "Rubber Man" skateboard style set a record for being featured six times on the cover of *Surfer* magazine.

Ian Cairns founded the Association of Surfing Professionals and was Australia's most successful international professional surfer. His peer acknowledgment came because of his aggressive power style, which tied a bow on his legacy.

Ian Cairns

Master Professional Surfrider

Ian Cairns was an international pro surfing champion from western Australia, who powered his way through the ranks of the world surfing circuit with deep aggressive turns that eventually led to a series of Hawai'ian big-wave wins: the Smirnoff (1973), third in the 1973 Hang Ten American Pro, and, most notably, the classic Duke Kahanamoku Invitational held at Oahu's Waimea Bay in 25-foot waves.

An acknowledged, assertive leader in professional surfing contests and tours, Cairns worked his way through the politics of various organizations by creatively directing pro surfing's international acceptance.

Cairns is a champion Aussie surfer turned surf organizer who has supported surfing's emergence throughout his career, much to the benefit of surfing.

When it comes to being prepared for the variable range of surf conditions on the North Shore, a quiver of equipment is simply a necessity, as Jeff Crawford displays.

Jeff Crawford
Master East Coast Surfrider

Jeff Crawford honed his skills at Sebastian Inlet in Florida where the lineup can be as aggressive as at any of the popular surf spots around the world. Born in Florida in 1952, he moved around with his family in his early years and got into surfing at the age of 16 in New Smyrna Beach. In 1971, Crawford won the Florida state championships, and a year later he was runner-up in the United States championships. He then worked his way through the world championships to the semi-finals in the same year.

After spending a year getting his bearings on the North Shore of Oahu, Crawford was invited to the prestigious Pipeline Masters, where as the East Coast surfer he went up against the legends of the Pipeline, Gerry Lopez and Rory Russell, and won. He was the first East Coast surfer ever to win the Pipeline Masters, and from there he went on to be invited to the Duke Kahanamoku Invitational in 1975. He finally hung up his competition jersey after winning world pro tour events in Florida in 1977 and 1978.

In the 1970s, Crawford appeared in a series of surf films. He was inducted into the East Coast Surfing Legends Hall of Fame in 2002.

Tom Carroll would leave a legacy in the history books as a full-circle power surfer. And he would also be known as "the best tuberider of his era."

Tom Carroll
Australia's Legendary Tuberider

Tom Carroll was surfing's first million-dollar surf star when in 1988, Carroll and Quiksilver surfwear signed a five-year agreement two decades after he began surfing as an eight-year-old in Sydney, Australia. With a successful amateur tenure, Carroll entered the 1979 Pipeline Masters as a rookie, making it into the finals. After surfing on the tour for three years, he won his first world championship in 1983 and his second in 1984.

Carroll was a natural, fearless tuberider who seemed innately knowing in how to fit inside and get out. His talent was to ride very big surf, something he could and would wrap his power around, and with that mindset, he became surfing's best tuberider of the era. As a veteran, he was a popular pro tour surfer with a sense of confidence and humility that made him approachable. So it came as no surprise that the Australian Surfing Hall of Fame inducted and honored him, *Australian Surfing Life* magazine readers' poll chose him in 1991, and eight years later Huntington Beach Surfing Walk of Fame gave him a place of honor.

Carroll retired from pro surfing on the world tour in 1993.

Champion Tom Curren is one of surfing's most outstanding stylists in a world of master stylists.

Tom Curren
Grand Master Stylist

Tom Curren has been idolized by aware surf aficionados, the surf media, and the mainstream media. From outside appearances, Curren is a mysterious world champion who set the bar very high with a riding style in the 1980s and 1990s that heavily influenced the next generation of pro surfers. Curren is one of those surfer's surfers.

The son of Pat Curren, a pioneer big wave rider and board builder of Waimea "gun" surfboards, Tom Curren began his surfing life at the age of six. From there, he began his amateur and then professional surfing career that extended over three decades, winning multiple major surf events throughout the world, and highlighted by winning the *Surfer* magazine Readers' Poll *eight years in a row* (1985–1992).

Curren has appeared in more than 100 surf films, ranging from the 1990 *Surfers: The Movie* to *The Endless Summer II*, and his career culminated in getting his plaque on the Huntington Beach Surfing Walk of Fame in 1995.

Rolf Aurness
1970s World Champion Surfrider

Ralph Aurness possessed a quiet, humble manner on land and an aggressive attitude in the water. He started surfing at the early age of 8 and almost immediately got into the California amateur surfing championships, winning the top ranking in the boys division in 1967 at 15. At 16, Aurness entered the 1968 World Contest in Puerto Rico; the following year he prevailed in winning the prestigious California AAAA Western Surfing Association Circuit.

Aurness always rode Bing surfboards exclusively, and when he went to Australia to compete in the 1970 World Championships at Johanna, he won with eye-widening speed against such international names as Wayne Lynch and Nat Young, riding a Bing 6-foot, 10-inch foil that was almost a foot longer than his challengers' boards.

Rolf Aurness was 18 years old at the time he won the World Contest. He then decided to hang up his competitive surfing career and never compete again.

Recognition of Rolf Aurness' world-class surfriding skills seemed to come out of the blue. Sure, he had the "good surfer" reputation among his peers, but there were some aficionados who pointed to Aurness as being "the best" surfer in the world.

Shane Dorian was ranked fourth in the world in 2000 yet admitted that he really didn't have the killer instincts needed to compete.

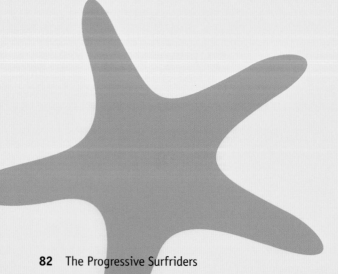

Shane Dorian
Master Surfrider

Shane Dorian is one of those surfers who, at the peak of his world-class professional career, was recognized by his peers as a master surfer among all surfers. Born in 1972 in Kona, Hawai'i, Dorian started surfing at the age of 5 and purposefully went from amateur *menehune* to professional surfer at 17. In 2000, *Surfer* magazine pointed to Dorian, saying, "Shane has the best reputation on the world tour, hot, progressive, utterly fearless" in summing up more than three decades of professional surfing.

Yet there's more to Dorian's story: In between the contests, Dorian really shone as a free-style aerialist, an extraordinary tuberider, and renowned world-class big-wave rider. This fact was not overlooked by the respondents to *Surfer* magazine's Readers' Poll, who voted Dorian as runner-up to Kelly Slater for best surfer of 2000.

Cheyne Horan
Australian Innovative Champion

Cheyne Horan was Australia's extraordinary and eccentric teenage surfing champion. He went pro at 16, and over the years his career went from astounding finishes then slipped to very low showings. Then in 1987, Horan made a comeback by winning surfing's biggest cash prize up to that date, $50,000 for the Billabong Pro. After that, in 1993, he quit professional surfing, with his record showing he had won 12 world tour contest victories.

Horan continued surfing by tackling the big-wave challenges of Jaws on Maui, and he took part habitually in the Eddie Aikau Memorial contest at Waimea Bay. Cheyne Horan won *Surfer* magazine's Readers' Poll in 1983, and when Quiksilver ran the 1999 Masters World Contest for surfers over the age of 36, Horan emerged victorious.

In 1984, Cheyne Horan won the Billabong Professional in Hawai'i, taking home a prize of $50,000, the most money a surfer had won up to that point.

Colin McPhillips
Master Longboard Surfrider

Colin McPhillips brought his longboard approach to surfing up to date with dynamic power moves usually associated with shortboard wave riding. McPhillips was born in 1975 and started surfing when he was five years old in San Clemente, California. In the beginning of his surfing career, Colin went short before he went long. As a shortboarder, he was successful in attaining a fourth place in the 1992 United States Surfing Championships held at Huntington Beach, California. As a longboarder, McPhillips was even more successful, winning the Longboard World Championships three times. In 2002, he took the Professional Surfing Tour of America Championship.

McPhillips, who has a lengthy record of longboard competition, didn't follow the traditional "flowing with it" approach to wave riding. He took up the shortboard ripping method with great success.

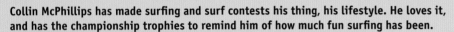

Collin McPhillips has made surfing and surf contests his thing, his lifestyle. He loves it, and has the championship trophies to remind him of how much fun surfing has been.

Gary "Kong" Elkerton
Freestyle, Aggressive, Power Surfrider

Gary Elkerton came into surfing with the eye of the tiger, which is really the only way one can make it on the professional surfing world circuit. There's no room for the timid. Although Elkerton was an aggressive competitor, winning the Hawai'ian Triple Crown series in 1987 and 1989 and coming in runner-up in the professional world tour in 1987, 1990, and 1993, he was really a free-style power surfer who knew no equal.

During his climb to prominence, Quiksilver brought Elkerton onto their surf team and exploited his nickname, "Kong." He was wild, aggressive, and young: the right surfer to appeal to the upcoming youth of Australia.

Among many acknowledgments, Elkerton was voted "Best at Sunset Beach" in 1992 by Australia's *Surfing Life*.

Gary Elkerton, Australia's classic power surfer, is shown here doing what he does best: dropping in on an overhead wave at Sunset Beach and preparing for his speed run. He was a master at Sunset, and his peers knew it.

The Progressive Surfriders **85**

Wingnut is anything but. He is a surfer par excellence—and has been one for a couple of decades. He brings a certain sense of fun to his surfing and lifestyle.

Robert "Wingnut" Weaver

Endless Summer II *Surfrider*

Robert Weaver slipped into international surfing fame as a star of Bruce Brown's *Endless Summer II*. Wingnut (his mysterious nickname) became an overnight surf star, and has never looked back. He was a "good surfer"—and with surf contest trophies credentials to prove it.

The success of *Endless Summer II* meanwhile seemed to catch Wingnut's attention, and over time, he participated and starred in multiple surf videos and also did the voice-over narration on several more. He turned out to be a real pro in the surf film media.

After flying high with the *Endless Summer II* job, Wingnut simmered down and teamed up with Robert August of *Endless Summer* and created a long-term and rewarding business relationship with Robert August Surfboards.

Of course, none of this could have happened without a little luck and if Wingnut would just been an average surfer. As a loyal longboarder from the first day he got wet, Wingnut has fine-tuned his surfing skills doing exhibitions for Robert August Surf Shop Tours, while maintaining a high level of professional longboarding viability.

Rob Machado

Progressive Master Stylist

Rob Machado, who was born Down Under in Sydney, Australia, started getting hot late in the twentieth century (circa 1992) and began winning a series of major surf contests and professional world tour placements that put him, and the new school of surfing of which he was a leader, way out in front of the era. The new creative surf crew compiled progressive acrobatic feats that took surfing into unexpected zones of possibility, yet Machado distinguished himself from those hot young surfers with an enviable "flow with it" style that reflected his confidence and composure on the wave.

Machado, a thin 5-foot, 10-inch positive young man, has been featured in 50 or more surf movies, including *The Rob Machado Chronicles* in 1996. He founded the Rob Machado Surf Classic and Beach Fair in 1997. *Surfer* magazine's Readers' Poll recognized Machado (as runner-up to Kelly Slater) in 1994, 1996, 1997, 1999, and 2001.

Rob Machado brings a sense of smooth style to the shortboard revolution that was earlier ushered in with the rip, tear, and lacerate motto.

As a teenage gremmie, Joel Tudor was mentored by international master surfers Donald Takayama and Nat Young. He soon emerged as a master surfrider in his own right.

Joel Tudor
Master Longboard Specialist

Joel Tudor, a Southern California longboard surfer out of the San Diego area, was born in 1976 and slipped into his future surfing career at 5 years of age, went pro at 14, and never looked back.

Tudor became the foremost longboarder of the second half of the twentieth century. Some say that he could be the reincarnation of David Nuuhiwa, whose mastery of longboarding and noseriding was legendary in the 1960s. Early in his career, Tudor decided to specialize in the art of surfing longboards and developed a style that was reminiscent of the traditional flow-and-blend style of the 1950s and early 1960s. This is not to say that he could not call on his power skills, when surf demanded it. After all, he's a shortboard surfer, too. Tudor has mastered longboards from tip to stern, with a classic, subtle style that's well balanced and effortlessly smooth.

It's easy to see how, with a garage full of awards and trophies that account for three decades of professional surfing, *The Surfer's Journal* would describe Tudor as, "the finest longboard surfer of all time."

Michael Ho

Professional Hawai'ian Master Surfrider Michael Ho, weighing in at 5 feet 5 inches and 135 pounds, was one of the first Hawai'ians to go pro and was born in 1957. Ho came out of Waimanalo, Oahu, and started surfing at age three. He began his amateur surfing career in 1970, and after running the gamut of amateur contests, he went pro. While he surfed competitively and did very well on the world tour, Michael Ho really excelled in his home surf. Over a 25-year span, Ho won the Triple Crown twice, the Pipeline Masters five times, the Duke Kahanamoku Invitational twice, and the Xcel Pro four times.

At the end of the twentieth century, Michael Ho was still competing successfully in the World Masters Championships.

This photo of Michael Ho was taken after he won the Pipeline Masters with a broken wrist, proving once again that champions are made, not born.

Derek Ho
Hawai'ian Master

Derek Ho could drive smoothly through the Hawai'ian barrels from very deep inside, through spit and spray, over and over again—Ho had wired it! And he did it with a precision style that supported clean, purposeful moves. After more than a decade of competing professionally, Ho won the 1993 world tour, by winning the last event on the tour, the Pipeline Masters. Derek was the first Hawai'ian to win the world pro title. Like his brother, Michael, Derek Ho gathered a bounty of international accolades and titles over the years: he was a world champion, a two-time Pipeline Masters winner, and four times the winner of the Triple Crown Series.

Yet Derek is always more comfortable surfing in the Pacific waters surrounding the Hawai'ian Islands, and he has created his legacy by matching up with the most powerful waves in the world.

Hawai'ian stylist Derek Ho was most successful surfing in Hawai'i because the power of the waves suited his fast attack and tuberiding skill, especially at the Pipeline.

Andy and Bruce Irons
Kauai's Master Surfers

Andy Irons, the older brother of Bruce Irons, was born in 1978 with his brother coming in a year later in 1979. Between the two brothers, they set down a maze of surfing accomplishments that boggles the minds of surf devotees. Although, like most siblings, they were quarrelsome, apart they were champions in their own right.

Andy and Bruce began to surf on the Hawai'ian island of Kauai, a rugged hard-core proving ground. Andy got wet at the age of eight, and Bruce followed suit at age seven. Both boys went on to major contest accomplishments after going through the amateur circuit. Bruce turned pro after completing high school, and Andy got his pro career started while still in high school.

Andy Irons, a 6-foot, 2-inch, lean young man, is considered by those who study professional surfing to be a highly skilled surfer, especially in the big-wave category. His range of wave riding included driving fearlessly into the strength and the power of the waves, yet he could adapt to surf smaller waves with creativity and aerials, also.

In 2002, Andy won the world championship, the Triple Crown of Surfing, and the Pipeline Masters. Billabong signed Andy for enough money to qualify him as one very wealthy surfer.

Bruce Irons, with a smooth surfing style, could ride the barrels of the Pipe with the most casual and almost indifferent attitude and then fly into the air sporadically whenever the wave offered an opening. Weighing in at 165 pounds and standing 5 feet 10 inches, Bruce won the Pipeline Masters in 2001 over Kelly Slater and then came back later to win the Gotcha Pro at Pipeline. Bruce got the nod from *Surfer* magazine's Readers' Poll in 1999 as the breakthrough surfer of the year.

Andy Irons won two major surfing events, the World Championship and the Triple Crown (both in 2002), prompting Billabong to offer him a place on the company's professional team.

Not to be outdone by brother Andy, Bruce Irons displays the height a surfer can reach if the conditions allow.

Kelly Slater
Quintessential Champion

Kelly Slater is the quintessential professional surfrider of the modern age. Slater represents the sum and substance of what a professional surfer has come to be and has to be in order to prevail in the wide world of professional surf competition. Slater's uncanny balance and innovative tuberiding has jetted him consistently into the winning circle for decades.

A nine-time world champion, Slater started his march toward his surfing career at the age of 5 in the small surf breaks off Cocoa Beach, Florida, where the need for quick moves and superb balance come into play. As a *menehune*, Kelly started winning contests at the age of 11, and he began his unparalleled professional title run at the Easter Surfing Festival in Cocoa Beach when he was 14. Not wanting to go pro at that time in his young career, Kelly passed on the early professional money winnings. Then, when Slater turned 18, he made his move by entering the 1990 Body Glove Surfbout contest held at Trestles, California, and he won the first prize purse. The game was on! The mega surf corporation Quiksilver spotted Kelly's potential and signed him to a sponsorship contract. From then on, he began winning multiple events that culminated in his earning nine world championships.

No one comes close to Kelly's professional surfing career, and it doesn't seem likely that anyone will in the near future. Rumored to have made more than a million dollars a year, if true, it makes Kelly Slater the top money surfer in the world.

Nine-time world champion surfer Kelly Slater leans back and enjoys the last of the backdoor's leftovers.

PART 4

LEGENDARY WOMEN SURFRIDERS

WOMEN SURFERS HAVE ALWAYS been there, usually hanging out on the fringe of the lineup, most of them hampered by long, awkward, and very heavy surfboards in the beginning. For a long period of time, most of their wave-riding progress was in the doldrums.

Along came the lightweight foam boards of the 1960s, and women's surfing began looking up. Soon the women were doing their thing everywhere, and although they were fewer in numbers compared to their male surfer counterparts, they were there in the lineup, maneuvering for waves, negotiating for their share. The shortboards that were created in the 1960s were the perfect vehicle for the female surfer. Today, the woman surfer is accepted as a "good surfer" and well respected for her skill and her love of going surfing.

Kathy Kohner
"Gidget"

> "My ego was never tied into Gidget. I was just a girl who surfed, and the guys named me Gidget, then I left, and everything kind of went crazy."
>
> —*Kathy Kohner*

Kathy Kohner was just a young gremmie in the 1950s who happened to surf into the beginning of surfing's grand entrance on the world stage. She was a "novice," as Terry "Tubesteak" Tracy described Kathy when she first entered The Pit where the Malibu crew held court. The small-framed young lady, who just wanted to learn how to surf, got caught up in what was later to become the carefree lifestyle of the "beach bum surfers," a movement that infected tenants of the stiff Ivy League, crew-cut, hard-working mentality of the American proletariat.

Kathy's father, Frederick Kohner, wrote up the surfer beach lifestyle in his book, *Gidget*, which became the Hollywood movie that captured the imagination of the nation's young, encouraging them to take leave of their boring disciplined lives and go surfing! Gidget went along for the ride and became famous for just being there, surfing, and driving up her homemade sandwiches to the Malibu Pit crew who adopted her as their "group mascot."

Tubesteak named her Gidget because she was the size of a midget, thus girl-midget became Gidget—then came the blitz. And more movies where Gidget went to Paris, Hawai'i, launched a TV series, went animated, etc., etc.

"Gidget" was Kathy Kohner's nickname. She was a young Malibu neophyte girl who got caught up in the exciting craze of surfing during the mid-1950s. After her father wrote a book about her life among the Malibu surf crew, she became the symbol of America's new pop culture.
Kathy Kohner collection

Marge, Candy, and Robin Calhoun
Surfguide's *All-American Surf Team*

Marge, Candy, and Robin Calhoun were the "first ladies" of surfing during the late 1950s and early 1960s. All of the girls were excellent surfers and contest proven, plus they were statuesque, pretty, and easy-going. They had all the ingredients to make for a much-needed positive reputation for surfing, the emerging controversial sport.

In 1955, Marge began surfing down the block from her home in Hollywood at a right-hand pointbreak called Malibu. Three years later, she surfaried to Hawai'i and, at 32, won the most prestigious surf contest of the era, the Makaha International. She continued on with her contest pursuits and surf lifestyle into the early 1960s with both of her daughters following in her wake.

The Calhouns went back for other Makaha contests where they placed again in the finals. Candy won the 1962 West Coast Championships held at Huntington Beach Pier, while Marge added support to the fledgling United States Surfing Association as secretary to the organization and also as its first and only female surf judge.

The most notable historic legacy the Calhouns left was their 1963 appearance in *Surf Guide* magazine as the "All-American" surfing team, where they were photographed walking down Makaha Beach together, looking like healthy, happy American surfer girls.

Marge, Candy, and Robin Calhoun were America's surfing sweethearts. During the midtwentieth century, they epitomized the spirit of surfing and brought a sense of legitimacy to a sport that was suffering from a mischievous beach bum reputation.
Marge Calhoun collection

Linda Benson
Legendary Master Surfrider

Linda Benson went from a young gremmie surfer girl of 11 years old, to a world champion at 15—a remarkable feat in any sport. In 1959, she entered the newly formed West Coast Championships at Huntington Beach. It was her first contest, and she won it. Shortly after, she went to Hawai'i and entered the 1959 Makaha International Contest and won it also. That same winter, Benson tried her hand at Waimea Bay, the biggest surfing wave of the time and considered still to be extremely dangerous. Benson did just fine making her bones at The Bay, with the surf media documenting the event and anointing her for perpetuity as a master surfer, a world champion, and a phenomenal teenage woman surfer.

Linda competed for a decade, winning the West Coast Championships twice, and in 1964 she won a trophy in the United States Invitational.

Besides being the first woman to make the cover of a surf magazine (*Surf Guide*), she was featured in several surf movies and stunt-doubled in *Gidget* and the "beach blanket" Hollywood releases.

In 1997, Linda Benson was awarded a spot on the Huntington Beach Surfing Walk of Fame.

Linda Benson was surfing's first female small-wave hot-dogger who could match spinners with the best. On the other side of the scale, Linda became surfing's first female big-wave surfer by riding Waimea Bay. *John Severson*

Joyce Hoffman
Legendary Hot-dogger

Joyce Hoffman first picked up her surfboard and went surfing seriously when she was 13 years old. Hoffman would surf for long hours every day, waves permitting, practicing and practicing. She was a very competitive girl by nature, and she simply wanted to win. And she did, starting around 1963, by winning the United States Surfing Association's accumulative yearly ratings for four years in a row. During her reign, Hoffman won the United States Surfing Championships, the Makaha International, the Laguna Masters (multiple times), and in 1965 she won in Lima, Peru.

Hoffman was recognized as a "good surfer" by her peers, and she projected the perfect surfing image to a world still largely unaware of the Sport of Kings. Joyce competed best in medium-sized California surf and was a smooth hot-dogger, which was the style of choice in the 1960s.

When she went to Hawai'i, Hoffman took on Sunset Beach, riding it consistently with local acknowledgment and then to make sure her legacy was complete, Hoffman rode the Banzai Pipeline and was the first woman to do so.

Joyce Hoffman hung up her professional surfing pursuits in 1971 after *Surfer* magazine readers had picked her four times as the "best surfer of the year." *International Surfing* magazine chose her for its Hall of Fame. In 1994, the Huntington Beach Surfing Walk of Fame honored her with a star on the Main Street sidewalk.

Joyce Hoffman was a great surfing competitor who worked diligently every day to prepare for surfing contests during the 1960s. The effort paid off when she won the world contest twice in a row, in 1965 and 1966. *Ron Stoner*

Margo Oberg was the first female surfer to go professional by winning a cash prize of $150 at the Santa Cruz Pro/Am contest in 1969. It wasn't much by current standards, but it was a start.

Margo Oberg
Quintessential Women's Champion Surfrider

Margo Oberg began a ride into surfing history with the evolutionary shortboard movement, just as the longboard era was fading from popularity. In 1968, as a young teenage high school student, Margo powered forward, winning the first few of many high-profile surf contests, the California AAAA Rated Circuit, the Hawai'ian Makaha International Championships, the East Coast Championships, and the premier event of that time, the World Contest held in Puerto Rico.

Margo's excellent power and free-style athletic prowess when riding Sunset Beach were respected and acknowledged by the boys in the lineup.

Margo Oberg retired from surfing competition before she reached 30 years of age, a young champion who compiled a worthy list of surf honors, including *Surfer* magazine listing Margo in the 1985 article, "25 Surfers Whose Surfing Changed the Sport." Margo was a fearless power surfer with a remarkable amateur and professional career bridging three decades.

Lisa Andersen
Champion of Champions

Lisa Andersen's surfing life started out bittersweet. At 13, Anderson paddled out and began surfing at her home break, Ormond Beach, Florida, to the dismay of her father. So, at 16, Anderson left home for California, a girl on a mission, setting out to be a world champion. Next year, at 18, she took first place in the girls' division of the United States Surfing Championship in Huntington Beach. She soon went pro.

After two decades of head-on competition, Andersen slipped her pro contest board back in its sheath. Lisa Andersen had laid down her marker: four-time world champion, six-time pick as number one by the readers of *Surfer* magazine, and voted Female Athlete of the Year by *Sports for Women* magazine. *Surfer* listed her among "25 of the Most Influential Surfers of the 20th century" and *National Sports Illustrator* ranked Lisa as 76th in its "Sportswoman of the Century" rankings.

With power turns coupled with purposeful speed, Lisa managed to smooth out her style and was rewarded for her efforts with a *Surfer* cover blurb that said it all: "Lisa Andersen Surfs Better Than You Do!"

Lisa Andersen left home and went surfing, leaving a note that said she wanted to be a world surfing champion. She later achieved her dream, four times over.

Rell Sunn

The Queen of Makaha

Rell Sunn, the Aloha lady from Ohau's West Shore, was known as the Queen of Makaha. Among many other accomplishments, Rell was a professional surfer during the 1970s and in the 1980s, Hawai'i's first female lifeguard, and the founder of the Menehune Surfing Contest at Makaha Beach. *Surfer* magazine labeled her "the sport's premier female stylist."

Rell made history in the surfing world, appearing in several core surf films and a self-documentary entitled *Heart of Sea—Kapolioka Ehukai*. The International Surfing Hall of Fame inducted Rell in 1991, and in 1996, she was recognized by Huntington Beach's Walk of Fame. SIMA, the Surf Industry Manufacturers Association, gave Rell its Achievement Award, and lastly Hawai'i's Sports Hall of Fame acknowledged her contributions by inducting her in 1977.

Rell Sunn is surfing's international treasure. During her tenure, she was a great example and a proponent of the aloha virtues of the Sport of Kings.

Jericho Poppler brought that excited, effervescent attitude she gleaned from her love of surfing into her competitive surfing and her support for its culture.

Jericho Poppler
Wave Dancer

Jericho Poppler, a "good surfer," started her surfing career in 1960 when she was nine years old and never looked back. Gregarious, pretty, and skillful, Jericho put together a competitive surfing career that spanned two decades. Her involvement in pro and amateur surfing read like a hard-core surfer devoted to wave-riding. Later, she became an advocate for saving the surf, becoming a founding member and director of The Surfrider Foundation.

Jericho came into surfing when girls weren't appreciated in the lineup. Jericho was different; she was fun, amiable, and held her own with the boys at the Huntington Pier where she honed her skills. Her attitude set her apart. Surfing to her was a stage made for dancing: her heroes were Rudolf Nureyev and Cyd Charisse, which truly influenced her riding style.

In 1999, Jericho was inducted into Huntington Beach's Walk of Fame, a fitting award for a surfer who devoted her life to supporting the surfing world and dancing on the waves like a "good surfer."

Rochelle Ballard
Master Tube Surfrider

Rochelle Ballard is by all accounts a gifted world tour competitor with fourth-place rankings in 1998–2001 to illustrate the point. Out of Kauai, coached and mentored by former world champion Margo Oberg, Rochelle came out swinging as a rookie pro in 1991. She was "hot" then and went on to win eight pro events on the world circuit. Yet, that's just a piece of her story. She's more than that. Under the banner of soulful free-surfing, she took up tuberiding (circa 1995) when her fellow female surfriders had not explored that option yet. Ballard fearlessly went into the bowels of tuberiding "backdoor" with single-minded determination, and exited with the reputation of being the vanguard who led the women's tuberiding revolution.

Rochelle Ballard, a Kauai Island regular-footer, earned a reputation for being the world-class leader of the women's tuberiding movement.

Layne Beachley
Legendary Power Surfrider

Layne Beachley, a power surfer from the beginning, skipped the amateur surf cycle, went pro in 1989, and won her first professional world tour contest in 1993. For five years, Beachley was a top finisher until 1998 when she came into her groove winning five out of eleven contests to take the world title. In 1999, Beachley made it to two in a row, winning her second world title and prompting *Surfer* magazine to call her "simply the most powerful woman in surfing today." Not bad for a little 5-foot, 5-inch Aussie from Sydney, Australia. By the time Layne moved on from professional touring, she had laid down a record that still remains remarkable: two Hawai'ian Triple Crown titles and five consecutive professional world championships, winning more than $400,000!

And Layne Beachley wasn't done. Hawai'ian big-wave surfing was in her blood and in her sight. So, with big-wave and tow-in legendary surfrider (and then boyfriend) Ken Bradshaw driving, Layne was whipped into a 25-foot Outside Log Cabins wave, establishing her reputation as the sport's greatest female big-wave rider. Australia's *Surfing Life* magazine's peers' poll pointed to Layne Beachley as the top choice four years in a row. And probably the best description and honor came from *Outside* magazine in 1998 with an article titled, "I'm going big. Anyone care to follow?"

Australia's Layne Beachley is considered by students of professional surfing to be the best hands down female big-wave rider of the twentieth century.

BOARD BUILDERS

THE ART OF SURFBOARD BUILDING is a strategic alignment between surfriders and their shapers.

Much like the relationship between the bike racer and his mechanic, the surfers and their board builders are joined at the hip when it comes to custom design and craftsmanship. It's the relationship that has produced the evolutionary progress of surfboard design for more than 100 years. Much like fine wines and their connoisseurs, the value of subtle surfboard designs and changes are clear, by and large, only to the well-trained eye.

What becomes obvious to the surfboard builder is that the design of surfboards changes measurably with the size of the wave and the variation in beach conditions throughout the world: different shapes for different waves and the surfers that ride them. Accomplished surfers will have a quiver of special boards to be pulled out for just the right surf condition.

The board builder is more than just a skilled carpenter. He is an artist and an ocean engineer of sorts. There's a little nautical engineering science involved, but mostly it's a trial-and-error process. The shaper has to have the experience of wave riding to be able to make a custom surfboard. Without it, he's working in a vacuum.

The board builder is high up in the pecking order of the surfing hierarchy. The better the shaper, the more he is heralded and admired throughout the surfing world. As legendary surfboard shapers create their board designs, the more they become recognized and iconized in the surfing world. Their boards, in turn, become coveted collectors' items, with price tags to go with it.

The legendary board builders of the twentieth century created the tools for surfing, and in those designs lies the step-by-step history of their contribution to the surfing world.

Tom Blake
Pioneer Surfrider and Board Builder

Tom Blake was one of the twentieth century's founding surf legends, who made his mark on surfing history during the late 1920s and early 1930s. A surfrider with impressive swimming credentials, he won the AAU 10-mile race in 1922 and beat Olympic champion Duke Kahanamoku in the 220. Further, in 1932, Tom was the first to paddle 26 miles from Catalina Island to San Pedro in California. In addition to his waterman achievements, he won the first major American surfing contest held at Corona del Mar, California, in 1928.

A core surfer, Tom lived a frugal lifestyle on a small boat docked at the Ala Wai Yacht Harbor in Honolulu, Hawai'i, while surfing at Waikiki Beach. The local Hawai'ian beach boys welcomed Blake with Aloha, allowing him to immerse himself into experimenting with surfboards and paddleboards, using Waikiki as his lab for the design and testing of his ideas. Tom produced some of surfing's original board-building concepts and eventually manufactured and sold his paddleboards commercially worldwide.

As a prolific author, Tom Blake wrote several surf books, the first one on the *Hawaiian Surfboard* in 1935. Blake pioneered surf photography from the water; his surf action photos were published by the *Los Angeles Times* and *National Geographic*. In 1967, Tom was honored by being inducted into *Surfing* magazine's Hall of Fame and finally got his plaque on the Huntington Beach Surfing Walk of Fame in 1994.

Tom Blake, surf innovator for a period of ten years in Hawai'i, tirelessly contributed original surfboard designs, water housing photography, surfing innovations, and in passing he carved in stone "Nature — God" as a reminder of his cumulative philosophy.

This photograph of Tom Blake was shot by Doc Ball at Palos Verdes Cove, California, in 1930. Ah! The good old days with nobody out. Clarence Maki rides wing. *Doc Ball*

Surf pioneer Bob Simmons was counted as one of surfing's original board-design geniuses, a legacy that credits him with the concept of foil and the lifting of the nose curve.

Bob Simmons

American Surf Icon

A lot of the laid-back beach bum image afforded to the vagabond surfriders might have come from the surf legend, Bob Simmons, who seemed lost in the intellectual mathematical pursuits of surfboard theory. Simmons had little use for the creature comforts of life: his lifestyle was roaming the California coast searching for surf in his dilapidated '37 Ford, where he harbored his sleeping gear, food, and tech surf design charts. Obviously, for Bob Simmons, as it is for most gremmies, surfing comes first and the rest is incidental.

Simmons was a goofy-foot regular Malibu surfer, who was an acclaimed "good surfer." His forte was in engineering the development of the modern longboard. Bob was by most accounts, an eccentric genius responsible for a number of concepts, like the first dual-fin surfboard, the Simmons "Spoon," and the first use of foam combined with balsa for surfboards.

In the final analysis, Bob Simmons was a pioneer grand master board builder, a surfing legend, and an American surfing icon. *International Surfing* magazine inducted Simmons posthumously into its Hall of Fame in 1966.

Joe Quigg
Grand Master Board Builder

The first half of the twentieth century was a time in surfing's history when the future of board building was yet to be discovered. It was a clear field for aquatic design and experimentation that was particularly rich for the meticulous shaping enthusiast. Joe Quigg was a part of the early board-building era that was dealing with a blank canvas. What board design would work best for big or small surf? Would a regular Malibu Chip work just as good as a racing design at Outside Rincon? These questions and more were what Joe Quigg faced when he started out shaping in his surf shop in 1950.

His innovations in board building were the appreciation of "rocker" and in narrowing outlines for speed boards. Further, Quigg is said to have built the first polyurethane foam core surfboard and the first all-fiberglass fin that was raked backed in 1947.

Considered to be a meticulous, creative craftsman, Joe Quigg is an undisputable grand master board builder of the twentieth century.

Joe Quigg is a master authoritative board builder who is recognized worldwide by fellow shapers for his influential skill, creativity, and innovations in big-wave models and modern longboards. *Darrell Wong*

John Kelly
Designer of the Hot Curl Surfboard

John Kelly will be remembered in surfing's history books as the board builder who invented the "Hot Curl" surfboard (1937), a revolutionary concept that has had lasting influence on big-wave board shapes and surfing ever since. When Kelly first became interested in surfboard shaping in the 1920s and 1930s, the designs of surfboard plan shapes were in their primitive stages. While different board designs for different wave sizes and surf spots hadn't been conceived of yet, it was with daring and confidence that Kelly took an ax and chopped his friend's beach board into a streamlined plan shape, with a round tail giving birth to a kind of stiletto shape that allowed for high speed and traction in big surf. The "Hot Curl" surfboard was born.

In 1962, Kelly again dove into the unknown and created the "Hydroplane," a surfboard with two planning surfaces, one above and in front of the other, allowing it to hydroplane, thus gaining real water speed in big surf. It also threw out a dramatic rooster tail.

Among his other accomplishments, John Kelly was a part of the exploring gang who discovered Makaha Beach's surfing potential on the west side of Oahu. *Don James*

Hobie Alter
Grand Master Shaper

Hobart Alter, a.k.a. "Hobie," will go down in surfing history as an acclaimed international surf icon. He was the Henry Ford of surfboard shaping or the General Motors of the surf industry. Whatever the analogy, Hobie was the standard used to measure the "who's-who" of board building. He was considered the master craftsman of his era, founding Hobie Surfboards in 1954 and working with Gordon "Grubby" Clark to develop the first commercial application of polyurethane surfboard blanks later that decade.

Hobie began his surfing career at the age of 16 in Laguna Beach, California, and progressed to place in the finals of the Makaha International contest in 1958 and 1959. He later competed successfully in tandem surfing events, winning the West Coast Championships in 1961 and the Pacific Coast Tandem Championships in 1962 and 1963.

Hobie Alter was honored with a plaque on the Huntington Beach Surfing Walk of Fame in 1991, and the Surf Industry Manufacturing Association (SIMA) presented its Outstanding Achievement Award to Hobie in 1993.

Hobie Alter at work. *John Severson*

"I got out of junior college and I wasn't really going anywhere. My father suggested that I should go into the surfboard business. I really didn't think about that. It didn't look like something [with which] you could make a livelihood at that time. A good friend of mine said, 'You make 200 boards for everybody on the coast, then what are you going to do?'"

—*Hobie Alter*

Dale "The Hawk" Velzy, far left, hooked up with Hap Jacobs (next to him) and formed a surfboard partnership that set the tone for the 1950s. Bev Morgan (center right) sold his Dive 'n Surf Shop in the South Bay area to Bill Meistrell (far right). Bill went on to create Body Glove. *Bev Morgan collection*

Dale "The Hawk" Velzy
Surfing Icon and Master Board Builder

Dale Velzy was the original "core surfer" and became the iconic model for surfing's salty image to the world. A beach boy from Hermosa Beach, he began his surfing career at nine years of age and quickly gained a reputation as a "good surfer." He could hang ten. Along with his genuinely engaging personality, the Hawk could sell surfboards (make that surfer-speak for "con") like a politician promising free beer. Velzy would use the mischievous presentation of a Cadillac salesman to convince neophytes of the quality of his boards. Gremmie surfers always felt good about Velzy's deal and would brag to their friends about being taken by the Hawk.

Velzy opened arguably the first real surf shop in 1949 and followed up with multiple satellite branches along the California coast. Along the way, Hap Jacobs partnered with Velzy for four years, countersinking their image as legendary board builders.

If ever there was a West Coast godfather of board builders, Dale Velzy would be the call. To name just a few of his innovations, he launched Bruce Brown's film career, surf shop team riders, icon surfboard labels, multiple surf shops, and "The Pig," a wide-tailed, easy-to-turn surfboard. The Pig shape opened the door for a quick surfing success that appealed to novice surfers and "good surfers" alike. It was one of the best-selling models of the time, sealing Velzy's legacy in the annals of master board building.

In 1967, Velzy was inducted in *Surfing* magazine's International Hall of Fame, and later he got his well-deserved marker on the Huntington Beach Surfing Walk of Fame.

Dale Velzy, the grand master board builder, was surfing's iconic core surfer.

Discussing his partnership with Hap Jacobs, he said, "I needed help in my business bad! I [was] behind in orders in those days. I needed workers. Hap made some good-looking boards for the Dive N' Surf. I made all of Hap's while he was in Hawai'i. He picked up on making boards when he got back from the Coast Guard. I said, 'Hap, you going to make boards for the Dive N' Surf?' Hap said, 'Aw, I don't know.' I said, 'Why don't you come with me? They're not going to make it with that dive shop. I'll let you in for nothing. You're a partner. Fifty-fifty. Come on in.'"

Dale frolics beachside with Billy F Gibbons.

Dudley "Hap" Jacobs
Board-Building Maestro

Dudley Jacobs, who seemed pleased to respond to his nickname, "Hap," was a gentleman surfer, proving once again that surfers come from all walks of life. Hap was a young man when he left Los Angeles to live in Hermosa Beach, California. In 1947, he took up surfing in the South Bay, and six years later, he opened his surf shop and started his board-building career.

Eventually, Hap earned the respect of the local South Bay aficionados for his genuine craftsmanship. That recognition of Hap's board-building prominence eventually spread nationally, and his production followed suit, ranking him up there with Greg Noll, Don Hansen, Hobie Alter, and Bing Copeland. Because of his reputation for quality, Hap attracted a team of riders who eventually became legendary surfers, including Mickey Dora, Lance Carson, and noserider/hot-dogger, David Nuuhiwa. Donald Takayama shaped for Hap, and Robert August of *The Endless Summer* fame took a Jacobs surfboard (and its iconic logo) around the world.

Hap Jacobs defined what superior board-building was all about in an unassuming, quiet-spoken manner.

A core surfer with a gentleman's persona, Dudley "Hap" Jacobs quietly and steadily built a respected brand name, Jacobs Surfboards, out of Hermosa Beach, California, during the late 1950s. *Steve Wilkings*

Dick Brewer
Grand Master Board Builder

Dick Brewer has been a legendary, leading, innovative surfboard shaper for more than 50 years. He is arguably the most prolific creative board builder of the twentieth century.

Dick paddled out in 1953, caught his first wave, then shaped his first board in 1959, which opened the doors for him to work his way up the shaping hierarchy ladder into the exclusive order of international master board builders, with a future lifestyle dedicated to board building and the love of surfing.

Brewer, a gutsy surfer, also made his bones big-wave riding at 25-foot-plus Waimea Bay. A goofy-footer with a keen sense of function, Dick did his own testing of his "gun" designs—a feat that ensured his reputation as a master class board builder.

A grand master board builder of the twentieth century, Dick Brewer will always be thought of as a creative innovator of short- and long-gun designs. *Tom Servais*

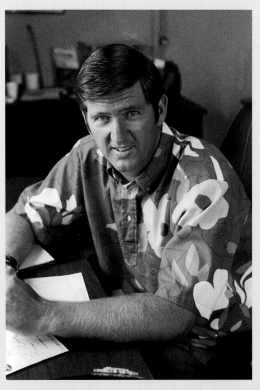

Bing Copeland
Master Shaper and Pioneer Surfrider

Herbert "Bing" Copeland was a shop gremmie in Dale Velzy's shaping room, sweeping up balsa and foam chips while studying the shaping craftsmanship of the Hawk. From that surf shop in Manhattan Beach, California, Copeland began his half-century surfing lifestyle. In his formative teenage years, Copeland traveled to Hawai'i and surfed at Makaha and the North Shore's Waimea Bay when it was seriously intimidating and still being explored. Later, just released from the Coast Guard and while sailing the South Seas, he and Rick Stoner dropped in and introduced New Zealand surfers to the newest Malibu-style surfboards. Leaving behind ten surfboards they made there as gifts, Copeland and Stoner are still remembered as New Zealand surf pioneers.

Always the gentleman, with a clever, stealth sense of humor and an eye for detail, Copeland created his international brand name, Bing Surfboards, with a reputation for timely, creative, quality surfboard manufacturing that has stood the test of time for more than 50 years.

Bing Copeland will go down in surfing history as a master shaper of the twentieth century.

Rick Stoner and Bing Copeland dropped by New Zealand while exploring the South Seas in 1958. While they were there, they showed the local surfers how to surf Malibu style and taught them how to shape the new-style Malibu surfboards. They left the Kiwis with ten boards to give them a start. *Bing Copeland family archive*

"Mostly I remember just hanging around and wanting to be like the older guys. Somewhere along the line, as I gained more surfing skills, it dawned on me that I was a surfer and wanted to be a surfer for the rest of my life."

—*Bing Copeland*

Mike Diffenderfer
Master Shaper

There was a Bruce Brown photo in Mike Diffenderfer's shaping room that showed him being shoulder hopped by Phil Edwards at Yokahama Bay, Oahu. In later photos, Edwards was isolated from the shot to illustrate his famous backside turn. "They never show the whole picture," has been Mike's lament. But when it came to shaping big-wave guns, Diffenderfer took a back seat to no shaper. He is an acknowledged master.

Born in Beverly Hills, California, Diffenderfer moved to La Jolla and in 1949 took up surfing at the age of 12. While still in high school, he shaped his first balsa board, and after completing school, Diffenderfer moved to Hawai'i to begin a long career dedicated to surfing and shaping boards.

Diffenderfer claims to have named the Pipeline for an early Bruce Brown film, and exactly how the name became an icon depends on which story you decide to believe. Was it because of the hollow shape of the wave or was it a "water pipeline" nearby? Only Diffenderfer or Bruce Brown really knows.

In 1991, the International Surfing Hall of Fame made Mike Diffenderfer a member.

And in his own words: "What actually works best is always the only priority."

Mike Diffenderfer, who made strikingly beautiful big-wave guns during the 1960s and 1970s, was mentored by Joe Quigg and Pat Curren. Diffenderfer made boards for some of the best surfers of the era, including Joey Cabell and Jeff Hakman.

Tom Morey
Master Board Builder and Surfing Innovator

> "Of all the things I've experienced, only playing music and surfing are tops. It's dancing on water.
>
> "Surfing has enabled me to express other God-given talents which pertain to design, fabrication, promotion, and sales. I am gifted in each of these areas thus born to be a surf equipment event guy.
>
> "I also want to say that I do believe surfing is creation's finest parable/teacher/simile for how to deal with life. It teaches how to deal with opportunity—when and where to catch what, how to stay with a foot ahead of the game, when and how to get out, and that the consequences of not doing some or all of this right really ain't so bad. There's always another wave."
>
> —*Tom Morey*

It's one of those unexplainable twists of surf history that goes unnoticed. Tom Morey should have got his due of surfing fame as a Malibu regular, but his surfing skills were acknowledged by the Pit, not heralded. Perhaps the reason behind the lack of surfing adoration was the philosophy that in Morey's early surfing days "contests" were laughed at, although he won first place in Phil Edwards' 1954 contest at Trestles. That was about it when it came to surfing contests, until he took another first place in a Malibu Club contest in 1990, which caused him to wonder if he should have gone pro. There was an agreement that Morey was a "good surfer," which at Malibu is as close as you can get to being immortal.

Morey was born in 1935 in Motor City, California, and then moved to Laguna Beach with his family before he began his surfing career at Malibu. From there, for the next half century, Morey became a one-man creative institution, supplying surf culture with a bounty of surfboard designs, aquatic engineering concepts, surf magazine articles, and products for a growing surf industry. The creation of the "Morey Boogie" was his most notable manufacturing success. Because of his bodyboard surfing invention, more people got wet, had fun, and got the feeling of what riding a wave was all about.

Surfer magazine anointed Tom as one of the most influential surfers of the twentieth century. In 2002, he earned a star on the Surfing Walk of Fame in Huntington Beach, and in December 2008, he was inducted into the Surfer's Hall of Fame.

Tom Morey is a visionary in the sport of surfing, exemplified by his Boogie invention, later to be called the boogie board or the Morey Boogie board. When it came to a multitude of surfing ideas and inventions, Tom was like Thomas Edison, creating more good stuff than you can keep track of. *Warren Bolster*

Donald Takayama was considered a phenomenal child-star surfer. He later became an international competitor and prolific surfboard designer for more than five decades, complete with his own surfboard company located in Oceanside, California.

Donald Takayama
Grand Master Board Builder

Donald Takayama jump-started his surfing career at the very young age of seven, surfing Waikiki Beach in Hawai'i during the early 1950s, and soon after, beginning his trade as a board builder. Donald was a preteen surfer when he saved his paper route money, caught a plane, and hooked up with Dale Velzy, the master board builder from the Los Angeles South Bay who had promised him a job when he arrived there. Takayama lost no time, shaping first for Velzy and Jacobs Surfboards before the two principals parted ways.

Staying with Jacobs, he introduced the Donald Takayama model in 1965. Soon, not to be attached for too long, Donald jumped down the street to shape for Bing Surfboards, where he created the state of the art, classic noserider for David Nuuhiwa. That completed, he moved again, this time to shape for Dewey Weber. Together with Harold Iggy, Weber's main man, they designed Weber's breakthrough "Performer Model." Finally, the timing seemed right, so Takayama moved to Oceanside, California, where he started to produce his own Hawaiian Pro Designs surfboards. Over time, Hawaiian Pro Designs has become a premium surfboard label in the surfing world.

Few great surfers are also equally great surfboard shapers, but Donald was an exception. He did both. Besides honing his production skills and creating surfboard designs that would eventually become collectible antiques, Takayama was also a master surfer who was quick and nimble, complete with iconic Island-style soul arches. Donald was one of America's best competitive surfriders with the record to prove it.

Surfer magazine pointed to Donald Takayama as one of the "25 surfers who changed the sport," and in 1991, he was inducted into the International Surfing Hall of Fame.

Reynolds Yater
Master Shaper

In the middle of the twentieth century, the first of the local surf shops began to sprout up. Those shops started in the South Bay and spread farther south and north along the California coast from San Diego to Santa Cruz. Reynolds "Renny" Yater opened his Santa Barbara Surf Shop in 1959 right in the middle, with Rincon and the Ranch in range.

Renny kept his surfboard sales in line with his ability to maintain quality. A conservative craftsman, Renny stood by his reputation of being a purist quality board maker, who made his mark with an innovative design he called "The Spoon." This novel board design featured a scooped-out, up-turned nose that contributed to easy swing ability and lightness in a longboard.

As an early 1950s and 1960s pioneer surfer riding longboards in California, Renny gained the reputation for being smooth and functional, which led to opening the door for his participating in many surf movies of the era. After all the foam dust has settled, Renny will go down in California surfing history as a master craftsman board builder and a well respected "good surfer."

Reynolds Yater came from an era in which dancing in the end zone simply wasn't done. Bragging was out; humility was the gentlemanly way of acknowledging success. Reny was naturally cool, and his surfing prowess and board-building skills spoke for themselves.

Mike Hynson

In Search of the Endless Summer

Mike Hynson carved out a legacy in surfing that is enviable in every way. As a surfer, he had the skills to be invited to the Duke Kahanamoku Invitational three times in a row during the mid-1960s. Mike also did a little contest competing, the Tom Morey Noseriding Contest (which he may have won, although it is still in dispute), the Malibu Invitational, and the Santa Cruz Big Wave Contest, placing favorably in all of them.

When it came to shaping, Hynson was a master board builder. Using his creativity, Mike's designed for the Hynson "Red Fin Tri-stringer" model that was so well received that under the banner of Gordon and Smith, Hynson put out two subsequent models, the "Hy-1" and "Hy-2."

Mike's place in the sun came with Bruce Brown's *The Endless Summer*, in which he was paired up with Robert August to star in a surf film about the search for the perfect wave that would take them around the world. That popular film put the final stamp of worth on Hynson's surfing legacy that spanned a half a century.

It seemed as if Mike Hynson was always on the cutting edge of innovative surfing. His exploration of new surfing spots, coupled with a tendency for the flamboyant, always set him apart from his contemporary journeymen.

Simon Anderson

Inventor of the Tri-Fin

In 1980, Australian champion Simon Anderson invented the "Thruster," a tri-fin short surfboard, arguably one of the most important, innovative, game-changing designs since the skeg. Simon's tri-fin became an overnight sensation, spreading quickly around the world after *Surfer* magazine listed Anderson as the eighth most influential surfer of the twentieth century with the "Thruster" in mind. Simon, a 6-foot, 3-inch surfer from Narrabeen, New South Wales, Australia—a big guy with a natural talent for power surfing—won more than his share of surf contests both in Australia and Hawai'i. In 1977, Anderson won the famous Bell's Beach Contest and the 2SM/Coca-Cola Surfabout in Australia. In 1981, he repeated those back-to-back victories and completed that year's pro circuit in Hawai'i with a first-place showing at the Banzai Pipeline.

In essence, Simon Anderson was a very good surfer—a superb, legendary surfer—and *Surfer* magazine agreed. In 1981, the magazine named him "Surfer of the Year." Later, in 1989, Australians called on Anderson to join their Surfing Hall of Fame. In 2001, just after the turn of the century, Huntington Beach gave Anderson an honor spot on its Walk of Fame.

Simon Anderson's tri-fin Thruster was a game changer for surfboard designs around the world.

Reno Abellira
Surfer, Shaper, and Shortboard Pioneer

There are many surfers who claim to have been on the cutting edge of the shortboard revolution. Reno Abellira, if not the first to go short, was certainly among those who saw the shortboard as surfing's next evolutionary step. In 1968, he competed in the world championships in Puerto Rico, placing sixth on his shortboard among longboard surfers from around the world. Some say he did much better than the judges proclaimed. The judges were mostly of the old school, where radical performances weren't rated as high as riding close to the curl for the longest period of time and distance. Nevertheless, the shortboard had arrived and Reno was a leading exponent of that movement. Although Abellira went on to win his fair share of contests, trophies, and titles, his most notable win was in 1974, when he took first place from "Mr. Sunset," Jeff Hakman, by half a point. The surf was a whopping 30 feet, and it is still considered by aficionados as one of pro surfing's most exciting finals.

Reno had his influence in the board-building world also. Along with Dick Brewer, Abellira explored the tri-fin and eventually morphed into developing the "Fish"—a twin-fin design that Mark Richards rode to fame and fortune.

Before hanging up his pro surfing career, he was invited to compete in the Quiksilver in Memory of Eddie Aikau contest that only goes on if the surf is 25 feet plus. At age 40, Reno Abellira finished 24th, beating one-third of the field.

Reno Abellira, Hawai'i's 1970s cutting-edge surfrider and vanguard board maker, was a leader in the shortboard revolution from the start. He even rode a shortboard in the finals of the 1968 World Contest. Here he is in 1975 on Oahu's North Shore with one of his prize shapers.

Tom Parrish
"The Man With the Red-hot Planer"

Tom Parrish began surfing on the South Shore of Oahu in 1963 when he was 12 years old. When he was 17, he picked up a planer and began mowing foam. Tom first shaped for high-profile surf shops like Country Surfboards and Surf Line Hawaii. Then during the mid-1970s, Parrish hooked up with Jack Shipley and the Lightning Bolt surf shop. Together, they supplied the best international surfers in the world with Bolt/Parrish boards. Tom became the "go-to" board builder in Hawai'i, which translated into positive acknowledgment and a sterling reputation.

Surfing magazine pointed to Tom Parrish as "the man with the red-hot planer."

Tom Parrish shaped his way up to the top of the ranks of worthy board builders by the middle of the 1970s, while gaining an international reputation as the go-to shaper in the Islands.

Ben Aipa
Virtuoso Hawai'ian Surfer and Innovative Shaper

Ben Aipa is the prime example of the pecking order in the Hawai'ian surf lineup. A power surfer with a semi-pro football linebacker mentality, Ben was able to dominate in the line. Yet his surfing was more of a combination of wave knowledge and athletic skill rather than brute strength.

In 1966, he made the finals in the coveted Duke Kahanamoku Invitational, the Makaha International, and in 1975, the Lightning Bolt Pro. With these accomplishments notched on his board, Aipa went on to compete in the contest circuit for many years and in his 50s was still riding a 7-foot, 6-inch board. *Surfer* magazine said that Ben was "the hottest 56-year-old surfer in the world."

In 1966, Ben Aipa took up the planer and began a half century of making surfboards, especially for the new up-and-coming hot Hawai'ian superstars. Consequently, Ben is better known for his innovative shaping concepts than he is for his surfing prowess. The double-point "Swallowtail" in 1972 and the "Stinger" in 1974 will go down in surfboard design history as hallmark innovations.

In 1991, Ben was inducted into the International Surfing Hall of Fame.

This photograph of Ben Aipa dropping in on a crystal blue wave at Sunset Beach mesmerizes, then draws you into the picture, into the trouble ahead, and into the opportunity beyond. Aipa, a power surfer with finesse, held his own on the pro circuit.

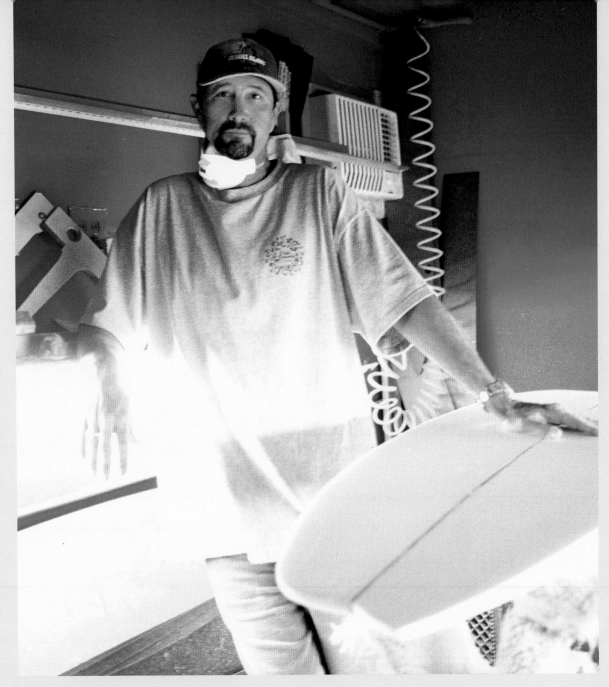

Al Merrick
Master Shortboard Builder

Al Merrick started surfing at 14 in 1968 out of Santa Barbara, California, just as the shortboard revolution was taking hold across the nation as well as around the world. Shortboard shapers began dominating the surfboard-building scene in the late 1960s and have never looked back. Merrick started his core Channel Islands Surfboards manufacturing in the 1970s, with his first team rider from South Africa, master surfer and champion Shaun Tomson. Later he brought on the local, burgeoning hot surf star, Tom Curren. Al's shortboard company joined their fame to become the world's renowned core board builder, and he became the "go-to" shaper for pro surfers. His boards were a composite of the current shapes of the era, but were highly refined and tuned to the ever-evolving demands of the new hot generation of surfers such as Rob Machado, Taylor Knox, and nine-time world champion Kelly Slater.

Al is a soft-spoken core surfer who rose to legendary surfboard-building status in the early 1970s and continued through the 1990s into the twenty-first century. For three years in a row, 1992, 1993, and 1994, Merrick was named by Australia's *Surfing Life* magazine as "the top shaper of the surfing world."

Rich Harbour
Master Board Builder

Rich Harbour was a soft-spoken, quiet, board builder whose national reputation for uncompromising craftsmanship told his story for him. A shaper's shaper, Harbour honed his craft over four decades, started surfing at 16 in Seal Beach, California, and opened his surf shop there as well. Rich Harbour Surfboards was a local favorite because his board-building skills were evident. U.S. champion Mark Martinson, Roy Crump, and Jock Sutherland rode Rich's longboards. The California Surfriders Club, rival of the Wind and Sea Surf Club, held its regular meetings at Harbour's shop. The shop was "the hub" for the local surfers of Seal Beach.

Rich Harbour's legacy can be found in his signature longboard models: the "Banana," the "Trestles Special," and the "Cheater," all creative innovations of the era.

Rich Harbour had an eye for shaping boards and an intuitive insight for promoting and piecing together one of California's best surf teams in the 1960s. He then backed it up with clever advertising. Harbour's reputation for quality manufacturing was comparable to the Big Six. *Ron Stoner*

Over the years, Hansen made several successful longboard models such as the "Hustler," the "Power Flex," and the "Master" with a who's who band of team riders featuring Rusty Miller, Mike Doyle, and Linda Benson. *Tom Keck*

Don Hansen

Master Longboard Builder

Don Hansen doesn't look like an outstanding surfer or a master shaper for that matter. He's handsome enough to be a movie star. Yet, looks can be deceiving as Hansen was a good enough surfer to make the cover of the 1962 *Surfer* magazine and was featured in *Surfing* magazine's all-star portrait cover of the prominent surfboard shapers and manufacturers and their signature surfriders.

Don was originally a transplant from South Dakota, who made his living trapping mink. At 18, he moved to San Diego and took up surfing. His board-building career came after he gained experience shaping in Santa Cruz, California, and then moved back to San Diego with a few stops in between shaping for Hobie Alter. Hansen's Surf Shop opened in Cardiff, California, and went past go right out of the box to a remarkable success.

PART 6

LEGENDARY BIG-WAVE SURFRIDERS

IN THE BISHOP MUSEUM ON OAHU there was an oil painting of a Hawai'ian riding a huge wave, 50 feet or higher, trying to escape death from a tsunami that was breaching the islands. It was an awesome illustration and an unbelievable story about how this terrified farmer found a plank and rode to safety down a wave that was said to equal the size of Jaws on Maui.

That illustration of the Hawai'ian farmer displayed the circumstances any surfer would face if he could possibly ride such a giant wave and, if failing, survive the wipe-out. Today, there are surfers that eye such big waves with a thirst to conquer, much like the mountain climber desires to scale Mount Everest. Daredevil surfers all, they lie patiently in wait for the storm swells to arrive, always searching the horizon for the biggest and baddest wave of the day.

Island legend points to Duke Kahanamoku as the first big-wave enthusiast. The Duke, it's said, took off on a giant outside wave called Kings Surf on Oahu's South Shore and rode it for a mile, coming to rest in front of the Royal Hawaiian Hotel. The next step for big-wave pioneers was to explore the West Side of Oahu at Makaha. Still not satisfied, the pioneer surfers went to the North Shore country to ride first at Sunset Beach, then, after they overcame their trepidation, Waimea Bay. Outside, Pipeline lay in waiting.

These were the big waves now described by purists as "paddle surf" to be caught and ridden the old-fashioned way, by one's own power: paddling.

Tommy Lee
The Cannonball

Tommy Lee must have been thrill crazy to be surfing Waimea Bay alone during peak conditions. It takes a certain amount of brave insanity to put oneself through such peril on purpose. *Bruce Brown*

Tommy Lee rode "on the edge" all of his life. It was his nature, and he loved the challenge. As a small-framed local boy, Lee began his quest for big-wave riding by specializing in surfing at Waimea Bay and became instantly famous for taking a seemingly destructive Waimea wipe-out, which forever tattooed him with the nickname "Cannonball Lee."

When asked about surfing in crowded conditions, whether it was safer or more dangerous, Tommy responded, "If you are going to die riding at Waimea Bay, it wouldn't make any difference if it's crowded or not." Which leads to a surf tale that was not widely reported. In 1963, there was an abundance of big surf going on off the North Shore of Oahu, so much so that a lot of surfers were simply burned out. Thus from time to time, the Bay was big and lonely. Lee would go out alone during these times, looking to catch a few waves before lunch. The waves at the Bay were perfect, 25 feet, classic giants. So, with nobody out, Tommy would nonchalantly start riding the massive waves, taking off on the far side of the peak for hours. Then he would go to lunch.

George Downing is pictured at Waikiki Beach after completing a paddling race, circa 1940. Downing became a diligent student and protector of the ocean and surf breaks surrounding the Hawai'ian Islands. *Dr. Don James*

Rick Grigg
Master Hot-dogging Surfrider

Rick Grigg was first a Malibu hot-dogger and then a North Shore big-wave hot-dogger. He just liked to have fun. Early on in his career, Rick distinguished himself as an ocean waterman who was able to ride Waimea as well as bodysurf it. He was that into it, and he was that good at it.

Because he was an outstanding North Shore pioneer big-wave surfer, Grigg was featured in several surf films during the 1950s and 1960s: *Slippery When Wet* (1958), *Gun Ho!* (1963), and *Golden Breed* (1968).

In 1966, Rick won the Duke Kahanamoku Invitational at Sunset Beach in Hawai'i, and he took second to Phil Edwards in *Surfer* magazine's first Readers' Poll awards in 1963.

Surfing magazine's Readers' Hall of Fame Poll pointed to Rick Grigg as the highest vote-getter in 1967.

Rick's surfing lifestyle speaks for itself. He was a world-class surfer in both big and small waves, and his love of surfing is even more profound.

Rick Grigg, who pioneered "big-wave hot-dogging," was America's master twentieth-century surfrider who surfed just for the fun of it. Rick celebrated by riding a perfect 25-foot wave in Waimea Bay. *Timothy McCullough*

George Downing
"The Teacher"

After Duke Kahanamoku passed, many consider Buffalo Keaulana and George Downing to be Hawai'i's greatest living surfers. Born in 1930 in Honolulu, Downing's career as a waterman covers the sport's profound evolution from redwood plank to the foam mini-missiles of today.

During Downing's childhood, the famous Waikiki beach boys were his primary instructors and the sand and sea his classrooms. Early on, he was a street-wise kid who learned to always dodge the other person's first punch—and make it be their last. George was equally strategic in the ocean, and soon his collected wisdom and smooth, measured style and courage in large waves was evident to all.

Always the entrepreneur, George ran the beach concessions at Waikiki for many years, turning it into a well-run affair that served the tourists, hotels, and beach boys themselves. During those years, he both met and was mentored by many famous personalities from all walks of life whom he taught about the ocean—and who in turn told him of their games. Due to George's savvy and attractive style, he was offered opportunities in their endeavors, but George always chose the ocean.

In his twenties, Downing traveled to Peru, surfing in their championships and becoming life-long friends with both poor and wealthy surfers of that country.

A past Makaha Champion himself and later an advisor and mentor to Hawai'ian surfing youth during international competitions, in the late 1980s, George created the Quiksilver in Memory of Eddie Aikau Contest at Waimea Bay, a big-wave riding event that requires 25+ surf, and has served as director since its inception, making the critical go-no-go call each year.

In his later years, George has acted as a tireless defender of his beloved island's waves and beaches via Save Our Surf.

In his significant wake, George Downing leaves the sport a legacy formed by his uniquely compassionate, human level understanding of the ocean's life lessons. Both of George's sons are supremely handsome, skilled, and artful champion watermen in their own rights and as such, carry on the family tradition.

Legendary Big-wave Surfriders **139**

Greg "Da Bull" Noll

Legendary Big-wave Pioneer

Greg Noll would be sitting nervously in his surf shop in Manhattan Beach waiting for a call from Hawai'i on whether he should book a flight to the islands or not. If the forecast was for big waves at Waimea Bay, he'd go, but then the surf would have to be at least 25-feet-plus for him to make the trip.

Greg was usually out of the water in Hermosa Beach, tending to his surfing enterprises, so he had no time to really get in shape. California rarely, if ever, got really big surf anyway. Yet, when the call came through from Oahu, Greg was off like a fireman, speeding straight to the North Shore and the Bay, ready or not.

While huddling in the lineup with the exclusive big-wave riders' club, Greg would keep an eye on the horizon, watching for the biggest and baddest wave of the set. Once spotted, Noll would quickly leave the pack and paddle seaward to intercept the rogue waves. There, powered by his aggressive resolve and out of shape, Greg would hyperventilate, begin pumping himself up, then pivoting, he'd begin to dig deep into and down the face of the wave. No one could miss "Da Bull's" rides at Waimea Bay. He would always raise his arm into the air, touchdown style, after a successful ride. Of course, (tongue in cheek) he always sported jailhouse striped trunks just to be sure he was noticed.

Greg "Da Bull" Noll was determined to ride the biggest of the biggest waves. It was his goal and ultimately, his legacy.
John Severson

Buzzy Trent
Pioneer Big-wave Specialist

"Big waves aren't measured in feet but rather increments of fear," quipped Buzzy Trent. In the 1950s, riding monster waves and getting wiped out was steeped with awe and fear. Those who led the charge to ride the biggest mountains were few in number and a closely knit group. Buzzy was a powerful big-wave surfrider and recognized by those in the pack as a leader, the godfather in the search for giant waves. He was known as a surfer who was dedicated to riding 20-foot-plus waves at Makaha and Waimea and was simply not interested in anything smaller.

In 1966, *International Surfing* magazine inducted Buzzy into its Surfing Hall of Fame. He never won a contest; he was a free-style soul surfer who only liked to ride big surf.

Buzzy was an outstanding athlete who could run the 100-yard dash in 10.1 seconds, was an all-state high school football fullback in California, and a master big-wave pioneer in the 1950s and early 1960s. *Walter Hoffman collection*

"My love of the ocean . . . it's my life support to keep me young and healthy. I love the nature, freedom, speed, power, beauty. Diving and surfing just make me happy and free with the ocean. Just being in the ocean is beautiful. From the very first wave caught, I was hooked and that stoke has never left. I like to do other activities like dive, fish, and swim, but I love to surf. Surfing gives me a sense of dominion, grace, poise, and balance. It gives physical activity and camaraderie. It offers a sense of release; all I have to do is turn to face the horizon, let my mind go, and I could be 1,000 miles away on a tropical beach with no one out. To me, it remains a vital activity of my life with no end in sight."

—*Walter Hoffman*

Walter Hoffman
Pioneer Big-wave Surfrider

In 1948, just after World War II, Walter Hoffman, on his very first day in Hawai'i surfed 10-foot waves at Waikiki, just off Diamond Head. It was the start of the core surfer's lifetime saga of chasing waves. The mixing of freedom and work is always a tough compromise, especially when the surf is up, which is always the dilemma. Walter found himself on that fateful day at Diamond Head when he fell in love with surfing, never again to be free from the desire to get back to the ocean and search for big waves. It became Hoffman's quest in life, starting with being a part of the crew that began pioneering Makaha Beach and eventually going on to the North Shore. He was a surfer first and a businessman out of necessity, and he designed the two to work out splendidly.

As Walter's luck would have it, his mother was in love with the ocean. She was a good swimmer, which led to Hoffman's father buying a cottage in Laguna Beach, thus rooting Hoffman in the ambience of the beach lifestyle. At 16, Walter began surfing at Malibu, California, alongside iconic Malibu surfers Peter Cole, Matt Kivlin, and Joe Quigg. It was there that he developed the skills that would take him up the scale to the bigger waves of Hawai'i. Big-wave riding was Hoffman's forte. He was built for it physically and mentally, and he simply loved riding big surf best.

The Surf Industry Manufacturers Association (SIMA) gave Walter Hoffman its Waterman Achievement Award in 1995.

Walter Hoffman arguably started the California Surf Rush to Oahu after mailing home to his brother, Flippy, his homemade 8mm surf film. After viewing Hoffman's powerful surfing through 15-foot waves at Makaha, Flippy and Buzzy Trent packed up and joined Walter on the beach.
Walter Hoffman collection

Fred Hemmings
Hawai'i's World Champion

In 1968, Hawai'i's Fred Hemmings won the World Surfing Championships in Puerto Rico. It was the end of the era where riding as close to the critical part of the wave for the longest distance was the determining factor for winning. The new breed of surfer favored ripping the waves by riding out from the most critical part of the wave and then cutting back radically to return into the folding wave before quickly powering out again. If conditions warranted it, the surfer would then repeat the action. It was a fitting end of one way of judging contest surfing and the beginning of another. Hawai'i's Fred Hemmings had won the world contest to the amazement of everyone at the Puerto Rico event except Hemmings, who calculated and planned how to win and did so with ease.

Ironically, Fred stopped participating in contest surfing in 1969. In 1971, he created the Pipeline Masters, an event that has stood the test of time. Five years later, he founded International Professional Surfing and organized the first world surfing contest circuit. After that, he started the Triple Crown of Surfing, a series of contests on the North Shore that take place at Haleiwa, Sunset Beach, and the Banzai Pipeline.

No one blinked when Fred was recognized as the father of professional surfing. He earned it and deserved the title.

International Surfing magazine pointed to Hemmings as Hawai'i's top vote winner in its 1967 Hall of Fame awards, and in 1991, he was inducted into the International Hall of Fame. Hemmings is a master big-wave surfer and surfing aficionado who paved the way for the sport of surfing's worldwide acceptance.

Fred Hemmings won the 1968 World Surfing Championship in Puerto Rico against an international field of champions composed of Midget Farrelly, Russell Hughes, Reno Abellira, Nat Young, and Mike Doyle.

Peter Cole
Pioneer Big-wave Surfrider

Big-wave riding in the 1950s and 1960s was the perfect time and place for Peter Cole to enter the surfing world. The big-wave surfboards were big, heavy, and difficult to turn. You had to be strong and skilled in order to do much more than survive. Peter, a 6-foot, 4-inch water-polo player and a nationally ranked free-style swimmer, won the Makaha International contest on Oahu's West Shore. He was perfectly suited to explore the North Shore, especially Waimea Bay. When the surf got really big at Waimea, the crowd thinned out, leaving a crew of notables like Greg Noll, Pat Curren, Ricky Grigg, Walter Hoffman, Buzzy Trent, Tommy Lee, and Charlie Galento. Cole was always in the lineup and, like Noll and Curren, waited patiently for the biggest waves.

Although Peter won the 1958 Makaha International, he always felt that contests went against the principle of having fun, which was in Cole's mind what surfing was all about.

Peter still surfs at Sunset Beach to the applause of a new generation in the lineup. He gave up riding Waimea Bay in 1995 after surfing it for a half century.

Pat Curren

Grand Master Shaper of Guns

Pat Curren gained his reputation by building big-wave specialty guns for Waimea Bay, surfing the biggest waves of the era, and not saying much. He became the most outstanding, acknowledged surfrider of the late 1950s and was a part of the crew that first rode Waimea that memorable day in the winter of 1957.

Curren never showed any real interest in the surf media and for the most part shunned any commercial opportunities except for making his classic "stiletto guns," which cost around $3,500 in 1996. Later, the price went up to $10,000 per board when he decided to make only a few each year.

Pat was known for both making fun and having a dry sense of humor. In one incident he secretly started an oil painting on the North Shore right on the beach, never allowing anyone to see his artwork. To cut a long story short, after the surf winter season was coming to an end, he finally had a "showing" to the curious local surfers, and unveiled a "painting . . . by the numbers." It was pretty good!

Although Pat was featured in a series of surf films (late 1950s to early 1960s), he never was acknowledged in the surf fame category, deciding to stick to his chosen lifestyle of surfing for surfing's sake.

Pat Curren didn't get into the fame game. He just made classic guns and rode them across the biggest waves of Waimea. *Bev Morgan*

Over the years, Peter Cole has become the active grand master big-wave pioneer on the North Shore. He still rides Sunset and is respected and welcomed in the lineup. *Warren Bolster*

Bob Pike
Australia's Original Big-wave Surfrider

Bob Pike, Australia's first big-wave surfrider, started surfing when he was 14 years old at Manly Beach, Sydney, Australia. Gaining early fame circa 1961 from Bruce Brown and John Severson's films, Bob took to big-wave riding like it was a needed transfusion, a calling, a philosophy. Yet, he was equally adept at surfing small waves, winning the 1962 small-wave division of the Peru Invitational, the original Aussie win in an overseas surf contest.

Bob Pike dropped out of the surf scene during the mid-1960s, avoiding its commercialism and returning to his surf roots. As Bob reflects, "If no one had ever known if I'd surfed or not, it wouldn't have mattered one iota. I did it because I loved doing it."

Australia's original big-wave surfrider, Bob Pike espoused the basic philosophy of the true core surfrider: "I did it because I loved doing it." *John Severson*

Eddie Aikau
Waimea Bay's Legendary Big-wave Surfrider

Eddie Aikau will go down in Hawai'i's surfing history forever linked as the legendary big-wave surfer of Waimea Bay. He was the classic example of the Hawai'ian approach to riding 20-foot-plus surf by dropping in with his sweeping turns, powering through the turbulence, then shaking off the residue, ending the ride with a sense of pride.

Aikau was respected by his big-wave peers from his debut at the Bay in 1966 and steadily became an interpretive force in the technique of how to master it. Eddie had his share of contest achievements reaching the finals six times in the coveted Duke Kahanamoku Classic Invitational and winning it in 1977, and finishing the competitive season with a world #12 ranking.

Eddie Aikau was lost at sea, attempting to paddle for help after the capsizing of the replica of the double-hull Polynesian canoe he was crewing.

In 1978, the governor of Hawai'i declared April 1 as Eddie Aikau Day, and two years later, a plaque in Eddie's name was placed at Waimea Bay.

George Downing introduced the Quicksilver in Memory of Eddie Aikau Big Wave Contest held at Waimea Bay, which is held only when waves reaches 25+. The contest has become a Hawai'ian tradition.

In 2000, Aikau was given a plaque on California's Huntington Beach Surfing Walk of Fame.

Eddie Aikau would go.

Jeff Clark
Maverick's Maverick

Surfriders innately share the awareness that the act of surfing is a personal and lonely endeavor. This understanding becomes magnified when the waves get really big and you are by yourself. Jeff Clark pioneered Northern California's Maverick's, a world-class big wave. To ride Maverick's just by itself is an amazing feat, but to do it alone and to do it for 15 years (as Jeff did) defies explanation or comparisons.

Jeff Clark was the California big-wave explorer/pioneer who singlehandedly rode Maverick's alone, a feat that will forever be his legacy.

Mark Foo
Big-wave Maestro

Mark Foo took to big-wave riding like a man on a mission. Armed with the ability to understand and work the systems of advertising and marketing, coupled with the drive to maximize its benefits, Mark went from a low-profile surfing professional on the World Pro Tour to a self-made big-wave pioneering career that brought him international fame. In 1986, he finished second in the Eddie Aikau Memorial Contest held at Waimea Bay, establishing his credentials as a serious contender on the big-wave stage.

Mark was prescient in predicting his own death on more than one occasion and was once quoted as saying, "It would be a glamorous way to go; I mean, that's how I'd like to go out." During the winter of 1994, Mark Foo got his wish. Wiping out at Maverick's in California, Mark drowned on a relatively small wave, and with his death brought international attention to the very real threat of surfing big waves. He was 36 years old at the time of his death.

Mark Foo took surf-chasing to a new level by first analyzing the winter storms and swell directions. Then, Mark would hop on a plane and fly thousands of miles to intercept the big surf wherever it would arrive—in this case at Maverick's, California's ultra-big-wave break.

PART 7

THE SURFING MEDIA

WHEN SURFING FIRST BEGAN to surface, there wasn't a voice to herald its arrival. Of course there were a few early books about how to surf and surf legends of the era. Then came the visionary John Severson, who with his *Surfer* magazine's publication almost singlehandedly set the stage for the surfers' image, language, indigenous art, and beach clothing, which in turn influenced our eventual lifestyles.

After that, and over the years, the surf population grew, and more surf magazines and books were created to keep up with the changing surfing times. Much like the girl teen magazines already in the market, these surf periodicals were geared toward the young male surfer.

Today, the surf magazines are part of the world that covers the entire worldwide surf spectrum. They are the reflection of the surfing era, and they still search, explore, and record the spoils of wave riders throughout the earth.

As hard-core surfers took on the mantle of reporting and distributing the history of surfing, they gradually became professional authors, then editors and publishers, passing on the unique surf language and photos documenting for the surf aficionados the surfing events around the world.

Drew Kampion

Chronicler of the Sport of Kings

Drew Kampion began surfing in 1962 and wrote his first article for *Surfer* magazine in 1968, just in time for the shortboard revolution and the social upheaval that made the 1960s exciting. When Drew was brought on to edit for *Surfer*, "the times were a changing" and so was surfing. Whereas in the early days of the surfer, the sport was comfortable in its own skin, just hanging out and laying back, real life was in flux. The world had moved away from crew cuts and natural shoulder suits to hippie dress and Nehru collars. "Do your own thing" was the motto, and surfing was ready to do just that.

When Drew took the lead at *Surfer* magazine, he was there to make a difference and that was to take the magazine into the fresh counterculture ideas of the times. Looking back, Drew made his mark in surfing by professionally getting into and surrounding the sport. He cleverly described the Sport of Kings through surfing events, contests, interviews, environmental articles, and portraits of the emerging surf stars.

Richard Graham

Media Pioneer

If ever there was a "go for it" enabler who seemed always willing to work outside the box, it was surf entrepreneur Richard Graham. A confident, positive organizer, he managed to keep a low profile that enabled his multiple surfing accomplishments to go unnoticed. Yet, like, the elephant in the room, Graham was there prominently in the forefront of the surfing evolution, busily guiding and instigating creative concepts for surfing contests like the Hang Ten American Pro and *International Surfing* magazine's Hall of Fame. Graham was a "one-stop shop" from conception to organization to execution.

Although Richard started his surfing career late at 18, after working his way up in the Peterson Publishing ladder he became best known as the editor and publisher of *International Surfing* magazine. During his surfing tenure, he also became proficient as a surf photographer, a journalist, a Hang Ten executive, a Lightning Bolt vice president, and the director of the "Expression Session"— Golden Breed's no-contest "sharing the waves" event that put a bow on the end of surfing's "just for the love of it" era.

Richard Graham was instrumental in supporting a young surfing world as it got to its feet.

Richard Graham was always ready for a good idea, and because of this openness, he was able to perpetuate some of surfing's best innovations during the 1960s. *Dick Graham*

Drew Kampion is a "real surfer" through and through. He has unashamedly loved the sport of surfing and supported it with gifted prose. Surfing is fortunate to have such an advocate to explain the nuances and spirit that reflect the Sport of Kings.

John Witzig showed his in-your-face style when he announced that the days of "Cool, flow with it" surfing were over. The new era of radical maneuvers was in and here to stay. The shortboard was the new stick, and there were few limitations on where it could go or what it could do. *John Witzig collection*

John Witzig
"We're Tops Now"

John Witzig was born in 1944 and began surfing in the 1950s.

In 1967, he authored a startling article in *Surfer* magazine that placed the spotlight on the major changes coming to surfing by way of the Australian method of waveriding. The Australians were not into flowing with it! They were more all over it with radical sweeping turns and shorter boards. This aggressive attitude was described by John in a straightforward, in-your-face article that spelled out the changes coming. Entitled "We're Tops Now," the article turned out to be true as well as challenging. Surfing quickly left behind the style factor and picked up the radical ripping attitude that laid the groundwork for the shortboard revolution.

John edited *Surf International* magazine and founded *Tracks* in 1970.

John Witzig will go down in surf history as the surfer who warned the surfing world that change had come and that Australia was responsible for that change.

As editor and publisher of *Surfer* magazine and *The Surfer's Journal*, Steve Pezman has guided the path of surf lore for more than three decades with a steadfast dedication to the basic principles that are the core and the spirit of surfing. Go surfing. Have fun. *Jim Driver*

Steve Pezman
Surfing's Master Storyteller

In 1963, Waimea was closing out across the bay when Steve Pezman wiped out while riding a 25-foot wave and was swept by the current toward the rocks on the far side of the bay. Mike Diffenderfer, perched on the reef above, pronounced Pez a goner. The fact that he survived still remains a miracle.

Born in Los Angeles, Pez began his surfing journey when he moved to the beach in 1958 when he was 16. The casual laid-back lifestyle of surfing provided a match for the romantic side of Pezman, who by his nature looked beyond the surface of surfing's glamorous image and saw a culture rich in nature and truth, a mixture of fear and beauty, a world to be explored. Steve identified with this alternative lifestyle with all its salty manners and humor.

After embedding with the Huntington Beach rat pack who controlled the Huntington Beach pier in the late 1950s and 1960s, and in between dawn patrol surf trips to Mexico, Steve took up shaping, drifting as a freelance shaper from surf shop to surf shop until he eventually opened his own shop called Creative Designs.

Once again fate slipped Pez a "Pass Go" card: after contributing an article on board design to *International Surfing* magazine, luck once again made its move. Pezman went from contributor to staff and then hopped over to John Severson's *Surfer* magazine where after a short stint, lo and behold, he became the editor and then publisher for the next twenty years.

Under Pezman's direction, *Surfer* kept its roots buried deep. Contest surfing was not what surfing was all about. Surfing was also a unique human endeavor, and it needed to be nurtured and respected for the art form it was. After all, surfing's message came from Hawai'i where "Aloha" was a sincere greeting.

Soon, surfing was overwhelmed with pure unadulterated shoulder-hopper commercialism, and *Surfer* magazine's new subscribers were into contests, pro surfing, and a mixing of street and surf attitudes. It was time to move on, and in 1992, Steve with his surf aficionado soulmate, Debbee, opened the doors of *The Surfer's Journal*, a real core magazine devoid of hype and devoted to the surfers who know the difference.

With *The Surfer's Journal* in place, Steve's editorials and choice of subjects reflected the authentic lifestyle of surfers' unique perspective about their values. The communication is inherently "surfer speak," describing their philosophy from the core surfer's point of view. Pezman relays these attitudes, with prolific Hemmingway surf prose, to all those who find the lifestyle of a surfer to be rewarding.

Matt Warshaw

Surfer, Author, Journalist, Aficionado

Surfing has been fortunate to have such gifted writers as Matt Warshaw. The sport needed to have itself explained, described, and praised, not by outsiders, but by an involved aficionado like Matt, who is also a gifted surfer. It's hard to imagine what people would think about the Sport of Kings if it were left up to amateurs, or worse, amateurs who couldn't define the finite differences and never got wet. Matt got seriously wet in 1969 and was an amateur contest surfer until the 1980s when he went pro. All his surfing experience prepared Matt for a surf journalist career that spanned over two decades. He started out with *Breakout Magazine* in 1984, moved to *Surfer* magazine in 1985, and then five years later took the helm of the magazine as its editor.

Over the years, Matt's penned a number of surfing articles and books, including the Herculean task of writing *The Encyclopedia of Surfing*, the definitive work on the Sport of Kings.

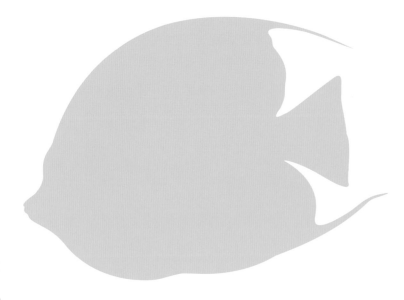

A journalist, editor, author, and hard-core surfer, Matt Warshaw underlined the lore of the Sport of Kings.

Sam George has lived an enviable surfer's lifestyle, roaming the earth searching for surf and writing about his adventures while profiling surfing icons—and getting kudos and a paycheck for his effort.

Sam George
Legendary Surfriding Journalist

Sam George started his surf journalism career by first going surfing in Waikiki Beach, Oahu, in 1967 when he was 11 years old. When he was 20-something, George held the California top ranking in the men's amateur division. Then during the 1980s, he went pro, sealing his qualifying credentials for his next pursuit: surf journalist at-large.

Starting out in 1982, Sam began sending in surf articles that got the attention of *Surfing* magazine, where he worked his way up the line and became senior editor for eight years.

Being a professional traveling surf journalist able to "talk story" with the world's professional champion surfers can't be a bad deal. Let's face it: It's got to be an ideal job for a dedicated surfrider with a nose for news. Sam has done a creditable job of doing thought-provoking surfing articles and contributing essays, and he has worked on surfing books and surf films.

Sam has made surfing his life choice and surf journalism his profession.

Paul Holmes
International Surfer Editor, Shaper, Author

Paul Holmes began living his surfer's vagabond lifestyle in 1962 when he was 13 years old and living in Newquay, England. Nine years later, Paul created England's second surf magazine, *Surf Insight*, and also took up the planer and began shaping surfboards. From there, Holmes spread his wings and began his lifelong world surf tour.

While surfing and showing surf movies in Biarritz, France, in the fall of 1973, Holmes was offered a shaping job at Keyo Surfboards in Brookvale, a northern suburb of Sydney, Australia. There, he extended his shaping career and wrote freelance articles until *Tracks* magazine hired him. He quickly jumped up to the editor's chair where he held sway for four years. Meanwhile, he took time off each year to be contest director of the 2SM/Coca-Cola's Surfabout, the richest event on the pro tour during that period. Been there, done that. Holmes jumped across the Pacific to California in 1981 and became the editor of *Surfer* magazine for nine years and, in addition, co-produced 39 episodes for *Surfer*'s ESPN TV series and started up *Beach Culture* magazine.

Life goes on, so Paul moved on—to work as marketing director for several surf-related companies such as Hang Ten, Gotcha, and ASR (Action Sports Retailer). In 1995, he went back to his journalistic roots as a freelancer and contributing editor to *Longboard* magazine. In 2008, he worked with Bing Copeland to produce the book *Bing Surfboards—50 Years of Craftsmanship and Innovation*. Paul has also authored *Dale Velzy Is Hawk*, a historical biography about the acclaimed pioneer icon of board builders in the twentieth century.

Paul Holmes lives a worldly surfer's lifestyle that has allowed him to surf internationally, always with his pen and notebook (and now laptop) at the ready, and thus make a living doing what he loves.

Paul Holmes is a surfer journalist who, by surfing and working around the world, has brought to history the authentic "local versions" of the surfers he has interviewed.

"Surfing is the most fun you can have with your shorts on, so if you can, why do anything else? When I told my English grammar school career advisors that I intended somehow to make a living at it, they looked at me like I was crazy. Maybe I was, but it's been a great ride and exciting new sections just keep coming up down the line."

—*Paul Holmes*

Craig Stecyk
Surfing Author with Artist Roots

Craig Stecyk is a 53-year-old Santa Monica/Venice Beach-based artist, writer, photographer, and contemporary bohemian personality with a personal foundation somewhat based in the surf/skate culture. He began surfing in the early half of the 1960s, and worked for individualist Dave Sweet, a pioneer surfboard builder and foam-core innovator.

Craig was a young confidant of the sport's "Black Knight," Mickey Dora, who may have been interested in Stecyk's extreme mix of intelligence and an amused, if caustic, view of mainstream culture's frequent disconnect with the surf/skate version of our life and times that paralleled his own.

In the 1970s, Stecyk authored one of the more seminal and procreative works to be published in *Surfer* magazine during it's 45-year run to date, a lengthy disarray of episodic, anecdotal, historically based fabrications that described with shards of wit and irony, a jumbled time line of Malibu events dating from the 1500s to current day, all titled "Curse of the Chumasch."

Craig operates mostly as a mystery man, admitting to bits of information about his whereabouts and doings on an as-needed basis only. His current status and whereabouts are unknown.

Craig Stecyk is an insightful, stealthy author and artist who has found the historical world of surfing and the street life of skateboarding to have intrinsic value far beyond the apparent surface.

Derek Hynd
Legendary Pro Surfer Journalist

Australian Derek Hynd possesses one of those rare combinations of skills that must be invigorating or at least very motivating. Derek was a professional surfrider with a high ranking on the world pro circuit and an at-large surf journalist, writing for *Australia Surfing World*, *Tracks*, and *Surfer* magazines.

Derek's professional surfing career was quick and surprisingly strong to everyone except Hynd. He climbed to 17th place on the world tour rankings before retiring after three years. As the Aussies say: did that, done that, that's that. Derek distinguished himself in the pro surf pack and moved on to authoring hundreds of articles on surfing.

Over time, Derek got into professional surf coaching for about four years and in 1992, working for Rip Curl wetsuits, he created "the Search," a worldwide promotional program that went to previously unheard of surf locations.

Derek Hynd authored a multitude of surfing articles and columns while competing and earning a No. 7 ranking on the World Surfing Circuit in 1981. *Sean Davey*

Phil Jarratt was known for covering everything and anything to do with surfing, including insightful profiles of surfing's icons, for more than four decades. He held down the editor's chair of Australia's respected *Tracks* magazine.

Phil Jarratt

Australian Master Journalist

Phil Jarratt is a prolific Australian journalist who specializes in covering surfing. Phil got started surfing in Wollongong, New South Wales, Australia, when he was nine. By the early 1960s, he produced his first of many articles on all aspects of the surfing world.

For three years, Phil worked with *Tracks* and Australia's leading *Edge* magazine before coming on staff, where he eventually took the wheel as its editor.

As an author with experience in profiling surfing celebrities, Phil penned and coauthored a respectable array of books with titles like *Mr. Sunset*, the Jeff Hakman story.

Australia's *Surfing Life* magazine selected Phil Jarratt as one of Australia's 50 most influential surfers. Later, Australia's Surfing Hall of Fame presented Phil with a special media award.

Phil Jarratt will go down in the surfing world as the journalist who underlined the substance of surfing through his articulate and insightful prose.

PART 8

SURFING FILMMAKERS

THE FIRST SURF FILMS WERE simple home movies shot with 8mm film sorely lacking a plot, if any. These movies were shown in private homes to surf devotees, usually about their buddies and the exciting surf they discovered. Later, storylines were created about searching for surf and surfing; they involved comedy stunts that only a core surfer would enjoy. As surfing grew, so did the movies. It didn't take long before the surf film was shown first in high school auditoriums, then in civic arenas, and eventually in true theaters.

The original, novice surf filmmaker usually was a Jack-of-all-trades.

He did everything. He organized and financed the project on his own, purchasing the cameras, the film, the lenses, the editing machines, and the projector, and he was the writer, producer, director, and editor. It wasn't unusual to see him selling tickets, too!

When the Hollywood movie *Gidget* was released in 1959, it was an embarrassment to core surfers and a lift-off for commercial surfing. However, the roots surf filmmakers didn't blink, and they continue making authentic surfing films to this day.

The surf movie, alongside still photography, is the historical record of the birth of a new breed of man that, by his nature, was divorced from the ideals and rules of social politics. Surfing was "the calling" and everything else was "dog food," to quote Tom Morey. Without the surf movie, the life and adventures of these young surf nomads would not have been brought to light. As it is, the surf film documented the surfer's lifestyle, showing the world this natural, new, and different way to live one's life.

Bud Browne
The Godfather of Surf Films

Just about all of Bud Browne's contemporaries acknowledged that he was the godfather of surf films as he literally created the concept of the surf movie. Bud financed the movies and filmed them from the land as well as in the water. He also directed, edited, added music, and did live narrations at screenings in high schools up and down the California coast. His films were original, honest documentaries of surf adventures using the home-movie approach with funny slapstick surf comedy to fill in between the surfing at the various surf spots in Hawai'i and California.

Bud's surf stories were told in a simple, nonhyped manner of what good fun, good waves, and the carefree, vagabond surf lifestyle was all about. His movies caught the imagination of would-be surfers and hardcore surfers alike and created a path for the surfing evolution that was to follow.

Bud created 13 full-length surf movies, all filmed from the water as well as on the beach. He also shot for MacGillivray and Freeman's *Five Summer Stories* and a Hollywood core film for surfer John Milius, the director of *Big Wednesday*.

Bud Browne was a brave man, an excellent waterman, a "good surfer," and a creative surf filmmaker. A self-contained gentleman, whose legacy was the documentation of the early pioneer surfers, Bud showed to the world what the free surf lifestyle was all about.

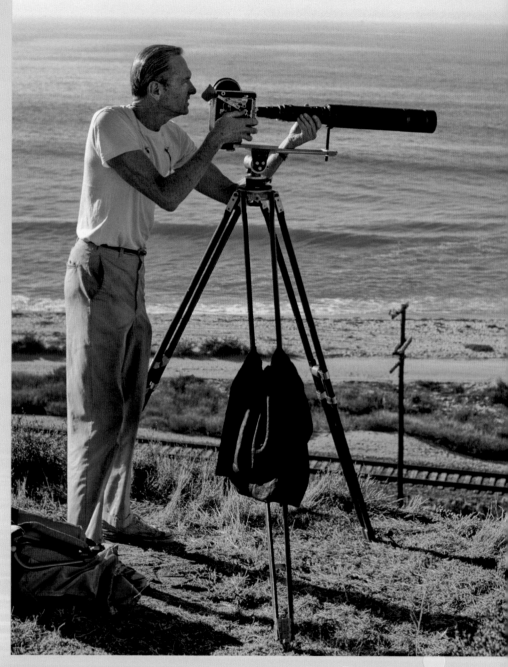

Bud Browne is acknowledged as the original creator of the surf movie business, his films setting into motion the lifestyle philosophy of surfing, which translated into "have fun; go surfing." Some think Bud started it all.
Warren Bolster

Jack McCoy is surfing's stealth international treasure. For four decades, McCoy has tirelessly documented the surfing world's heritage with timely stills and insightful films. It's difficult to imagine what surfing would look like without his contribution.

Jack McCoy
Surfing's Pied Piper Cinematographer

If achievements in cinematography were handed out in medals, Jack McCoy wouldn't be able to stand up straight. Since circa 1970, Jack has been in the lineup somewhere in the world, shooting stills and film. He has a body of work that would impress anyone who loves surfing and anyone who appreciates the waterman skills it takes to make his in- and out-of-the-ocean surf movies.

The surf photographer is probably the least appreciated member of the surfing society. Not that the work isn't creative and entertaining, it is; but people don't watch movies thinking about the cameraman. He is taken for granted. That's life.

Jack McCoy is first a surfrider with roots in Hawai'i and second a master-class cinematographer who leaves behind for future surfers their historical legacy. The surfing world owes Jack a long *mahalo*!

Bruce Brown

Legendary Master Surf Film Pioneer

Bruce Brown's surf movies introduced new surfers and flatlanders to the wonderful world of surf adventures. When America was still recovering from World War II and had embraced the conservative lifestyle dictated by an earlier Depression, people with tans who hung out on the beach were labeled "bums." Bruce's films changed that perception when his surf adventure films started to appear up and down the California coast and in Hawai'i in the mid-1950s. Bruce's surf movies were lighthearted with slap-stick humor because Brown was a lighthearted guy himself. His films had a homemade childlike adventure story to tell. Brown's low-key narration set the stage for the surfing mystique of the vagabond surfrider. Young surfers visualized a way of life that was free from the work-a-day mentality that postwar society embraced. Bruce's "surfing" was portrayed as a fairytale adventure you could step into and so drop out from the world that had too many rules. Bruce Brown was the Pied Piper of the surfing evolution.

Bruce made five films about surfing, two of which went mainstream: *The Endless Summer* and *The Endless Summer II*. In 1966, he was inducted into the International Surfing Hall of Fame. The Surf Industry Manufacturers Association (SIMA) awarded him the Waterman Achievement Award in 1994. In 1997, *Surfer* magazine presented Brown with its Video Lifetime Achievement Award.

Bruce Brown's surf films put a human face on surfing, a sport that was and is about harmless kids doing what kids do, having fun. *Surfer* magazine claimed that Bruce Brown was the fifth most influential surfer of the twentieth century.
Bruce Brown collection

Greg MacGillivray and Jim Freeman
Film Pioneers

Greg MacGillivray and partner Jim Freemen were the new breed of core filmmakers coming on the surf scene, following in the wake of icons Bruce Brown, Bud Browne, and John Severson. Greg and Jim were the first of the new serious students of surf filmmaking, and fortunately the world of surfing presented the living classroom for them to learn and perfect their chosen profession. Greg and Jim teamed up in 1966 after making surf films separately. Once together, they made several successful films, *Five Summer Stories* being their most famous. Their professional film school studies and their on-the-job filming of surfing guided them into exceptional high-grade filmmaking, bringing surf movies up to Hollywood's standards.

MacGillivray was one of the surfer cameramen for *Big Wednesday*, a John Milius–directed national release, and completed a series of short surf films before going to Hollywood and gathering Oscar nominations for best documentary in short subjects.

Greg was inducted into the *Surfing* magazine's Hall of Fame in 1967, and *Surfer* named him for the Lifetime Achievements Award in 1996. In 2000, he received his star on the Huntington Beach Surfing Walk of Fame.

John Milius
Master Hollywood Surf Filmmaker

John Milius was a Malibu regular during the 1950s and 1960s era, before he went to Hollywood. Thus, he knew what the true story was about surfing's devotees as opposed to what came to be the stereotyped image that the *Gidget* movie created and portrayed.

John was the director of a Warner Brothers film about the mid-century Malibu longboard era, as surfboards started down the path to going short. *Big Wednesday* wasn't accepted at first. But it later became a core classic surf film, probably because as time went by, the realistic view of the surfing's lifestyle that John presented wasn't that far off the mark even when taking into account Hollywood's tendency to overstate.

With his core understanding of the surfer mentality, John created the dialog for Colonel Bill Kilgore in the 1979 film *Apocalypse Now*, Francis Ford Coppola's gritty Vietnam War film. Told that the beach village that Kilgore was about to bomb with napalm belonged to "Charlie" (the Vietcong), Kilgore's reply of "Charlie don't surf" resonated throughout the surfers' world.

Greg MacGillivray, center, and Jim Freeman, in the blue shirt at right, were the creative second wave of the core 1960s surf-film producers. They took the home-movie element out of surf films and inserted professional Hollywood skills.

John Milius was a Malibu surfer turned Hollywood director who couldn't shake his love of surfing. *Big Wednesday*, a core cult surf film, gave to surfing a much more realistic roots image, as compared to the movie *Gidget*, which for some students of surfing was an embarrassment.

"Balsa Bill" Yerkes, circa 1996, pauses on a glassy wave at a secret spot in Costa Rica that Balsa Bill says will be known forever by the fake name of Manguante Bay.

"Balsa Bill" Yerkes
The Grownup Gremmie

"Balsa Bill" Yerkes is surfing's most devoted grownup gremmie. Deliberately lost in the surf roots of the 1960s, Yerkes stands stalwart against the gates of change.

Bill maintained that surfing was beautiful and, as far as he could see, there were not any good reasons to forget that and those that made surfing fun and special. One can talk story with Bill endlessly about the who's who, and what happened when, and surf music; he knows the songs, singers, and bands. He's a walking encyclopedia of the nuances of surfing and he's as hard-core surfer as you'll get.

Balsa Bill first went surfing in 1960 in the sweet days of Malibu. Hooked on surfing and its lifestyle, he proceeded to take part in the opportunity the surfing world had to offer. Besides surfing in the East Coast surfing contests, he shaped boards, manufactured an Eastern surfwear clothing line called Sundek, opened up a surf shop, and helped to start up the East Coast Surfing Hall of Fame.

Yet the love of filmmaking was in his bones. Before graduating from New York's Ithaca College in 1969, where he got a degree in filmmaking, Bill put together singlehandedly two films that historically documented the East Coast surf contests and the future East Coast Hall of Fame surfers. By osmosis, the Eastern surfer's lifestyle was also recorded, saving for future historians the way it was.

How the East Was Won, was Balsa Bill's signature film that captured the revolutionary contest billed as the East vs. the West. Dewey Weber vs. Gary Propper, which was when Propper won the East Coast, "busted down the door" of the negative rumor of inadequate surfers and dishwater waves. It was time to move on!

Balsa Bill was inducted into the East Coast Legends Hall of Fame in 1998.

PART 9

BANZAI PIPELINE MASTERS

YOU CAN'T TALK ABOUT THE SURFRIDERS who have mastered the Banzai Pipeline without mentioning the coral reef that lies 4 feet below the surface that the famous waves fall upon. The reef is unruly, sharp, and jagged with deep *pukas*— holes—strung throughout. If a surfer happens to be pushed into it, the results are not pretty. Over time, there have been deaths at the Pipeline—but not as many as there could be. Most surfriders who take on the Pipe are serious, skilled, and experienced.

A beautiful tubing wave, the Pipeline was discovered by surfriders who were exploring the North Shore of Hawai'i between 1940 and 1960. They didn't ride it at first because it simply looked too dangerous; for years it was avoided. Then, Bruce Brown, who was filming *Surfing Hollow Days*, and Phil Edwards checked it out in 1961, and Phil decided to give it a try. The rest is history. The Pipeline was rideable, and Phil rode it perfectly, if not without some trepidation.

Today, the Pipeline is ridden consistently, yet remains the most notorious of North Shore surf breaks. There are many famous surfers over the years who have ridden the Pipeline with success and yet there are a few who have excelled in their ability to rule at the Pipeline. They are called the Pipeline Masters.

Butch Van Artsdalen was "Mr. Pipeline." He ruled the Pipe by being the first surfrider to move through its tubing barrels and over its coral reef consistently with the classic style of a superb athlete. *Duke Boyd*

Butch Van Artsdalen
Mr. Pipeline

Butch Van Artsdalen wasn't the first surfer to ride the North Shore's Banzai Pipeline, but he was the first surfer to master it.

Butch started his surfing career riding Windansea, the hot surfing spot in California's San Diego area. He was a gifted athlete in high school, lettering in three sports, before surfaring to Hawai'i, where he mastered his switch-stance to such a level that he could do it at will even at Waimea Bay. Bud Browne and Bruce Brown featured Butch in their respective surf films, documenting his switch-footing skills and his consistent domination of the Pipeline. Simply stated, Butch had the Pipe wired. He was Mr. Pipeline.

Butch Van Artsdalen was a likeable, fun-loving surfer with just a tad of youthful mischievousness in his lifestyle approach, which may be the reason he became the first master of Oahu's Banzai Pipeline.

John Peck
Backside Pipemaster

John Peck broke onto the surf scene in 1963, when he grabbed a rail at the Banzai Pipeline and was immortalized in the era's surf movies *Walk on the Wet Side*, Bud Browne's *Gun Ho!* and John Severson's *The Angry Sea*. Dr. Don James was also there, photographing John deep inside the Pipe during those classic days when Butch Van Artsdalen was trading tubes with Peck. When the Dr. James poster came out, Peck's rail-grab became the notable ride of the year earning him a place in Pipeline history as one of its few masters.

John won a few contests, which gave him enough stature to parlay a sponsorship with Tom Morey and Karl Pope, board makers from Ventura, California. There he worked out the design for his signature model, the "Penetrator," a board that is unusual in that it could perform well as a speed design coupled with a noseriding feature.

Eventually, John grew a beard, kept his warm smile, and entered into the spiritual world, still surfing and shaping like the true grassroots surfer he is.

John Peck created his legacy on New Year's Day 1963 when he grabbed a rail at the Pipeline going backside and began riding with confidence and dominance at a break that still was thought too dangerous to surf.

SURFER | BI-MONTHLY
A JOHN SEVERSON PUBLICATION
APRIL-MAY VOLUME 4 No.2/75¢
THE INTERNATIONAL SURFING MAGAZINE

JOHN PECK · BANZAI PIPELINE · HAWAII

During the shortboard revolution, Jock Sutherland moved from mastering the longboard to adapting the shortboard to the Pipeline. Jock took his place in the lineup after Butch Van Artsdalen and before Rory Russell and Gerry Lopez. *Ron Stoner*

Jock Sutherland
Pipeline Master

Switch-foot surfer Jock Sutherland joined the 1960s decade of hot young surfers who made up a magical era of innovative surfing performance and board building. Around the world, surfing was coming into being, and the surfers of that era were finding fresh areas in and on the waves to explore more than at any time previously. With the advent of light foam boards going shorter, radical maneuverability came into play. At the same time, with the introduction of skateboarding, young skateboarders showed the kind of dominance over their boards that influenced the surfers of the day, raising the curtain on radical cutbacks, tuberiding, and rolling coaster feats.

When Jock began riding his shortboard at the Pipeline, it quickly became evident that he had figured the place out. And he was the newly acknowledged Pipeline master falling in between Butch Van Artsdalen and Gerry Lopez. If Sutherland wasn't the surfer who introduced the shortboard to Pipe, he should have been. His ability to take his new rocket-shaped, lightweight missiles into the Pipe must have been as exhilarating as the possibilities were endless.

Jock won his share of accolades and awards for his surfing skills. He surprisingly dropped out of the lineup and joined the United States Army in 1970. After serving two years, surfing had moved on. When he returned, although he was still surfing, times had changed. Upon reviewing Jock's accomplishments, his legacy is impressive. He finished second behind Australia champion Nat Young at the 1966 San Diego World Contest, won the Peru Invitational in 1967, and later that year won the Duke Kahanamoku Invitational.

Jock Sutherland, the most notable all-around switch-footer, became one of the surfing world's top surfriders.

Gerry Lopez
Legendary Pipeline Master

In the history of human endeavors, periodically there comes along a rare and clear solitary distinction among the many. In essence, this book is about those who made a difference. Gerry Lopez is one of those surfers who, with universal peer agreement, is considered a legendary twentieth-century surfing icon.

In the formative years of surfing there was a mutual appreciation, a bonding among surfers, based on the sharing of the waves with each other, enjoying it as if it were your own. During that era there wasn't a prevailing competitive attitude; there wasn't good, better, best, envy. Surfing was not a game where something was better than something else. What surfing was then in its purist form, was a ballet, with deference to the sea, a skillful dance on the beautiful wave, a twentieth-century art form.

Gerry Lopez was the embodiment of that era: He surfed with a Zenlike style with the least amount of unnecessary movement to complete the act. His dance at the Pipeline depicted his ability to make it look perfect by defining the classic approach to mastering the most challenging wave in the world—the Banzai Pipeline.

Gerry Lopez had mastered the Pipeline to such an extent that he felt assured that it made a good dancing partner.

Rory Russell
"The Dog"

Rory Russell was the epitome of the happy-go-lucky surfer during the last carefree days of the revolutionary 1960s. "The Dog," as Rory was affectionately known, could hold court into the wee hours. And when the sun rose, so did Rory, who would be the first in the line up if the surf was up.

Rory was an excellent all around athlete, so he surprised no one when he went pro in 1976 in the first year of the circuit. He finished eighth two years in a row. Yet his claim to fame was his domination of the Pipeline contest for five years where he captured two firsts, three seconds, and a third.

The Dog and Gerry Lopez, Rory's Pipeline buddy, were given all kinds of duo nicknames, such as Batman and Robin. But Rory's style was a more academic power style than Gerry's; Rory's attitude was to drive through the tube without a lot of setting up or stalling.

During the 1980s, Rory headed up a global team of surfers who rode for Lighting Bolt surfwear, where he became the official ambassador of goodwill. When that era passed, Rory eventually taught surfing on the Big Island and picked up his shaping vocation, making signature Lightning Bolt surfboards.

Rory Russell has always gone by the nickname "The Dog," an affectionate name that explains a lot of things, depending on one's point of view. Generally, it refers to his open, friendly manner while enjoying a good party. However, one may interpret him differently in the lineup.

PART 10

THE SURF CULTURE

SURFING'S SURF CULTURE IS **what takes place after surfers have gone** **surfing and gotten out of the water.** When the surf is flat, blown out, or simply victory-at-sea, it's back to enjoying the surfing life's leftovers— the everything else that's about surfing.

First, surfers search for surf even if there's none to be had. Then they open surf shops, blow foam, shape and glass boards, start magazines and surfwear clothing companies, organize games, and put on surf contests, stuff like that. It's fun, creative, and doesn't seem like "real work." Yet, always in the back of the surfer's mind, everything is temporary, and not much matters until the next good swell. Then it's "Gone Surfing."

This single-minded devotion to the actual surfing is what makes the surf culture counter to the mainstream society, which is devoted to a work ethic for its own sake. It's a simple truth for surfers: the surf lifestyle has viability, and it's the best way to spend your time on earth.

Lewis "Hoppy" Swarts

Pioneer Surfrider, First President of USSA

Born in 1916, Lewis Swarts always went by his nickname "Hoppy" after movie cowboy "Hopalong" Cassidy. He began surfing at 14 at Hermosa Beach, California. In 1935, he joined the Palos Verdes Surfing Club and became an active competitor in the surfing contest of the era, the Pacific Coast Surfriding Championship.

In the early 1960s, because the rowdy young surf gremmies were feeling a little too "free," beach towns on both the East and West Coasts were preparing to set down ordinances that would ban surfing on their beaches and thus prevent social unrest.

Hoppy became the president of the United States Surfing Association (USSA), which was formed for the purpose of cleaning up the surfer image through surfing competition. The concept was if the contests could prove to be legitimate endeavors, giving surfers a game that could be understood with awards, trophies, and the like, then surfing would take on a real, positive sports image that could be understood by the towns' councils. It worked. Along with surfers wearing coats and ties with crewcuts, the problem with surfing and surfers subsided.

The USSA eventually morphed into regional chapters, and Hoppy continued to support surfing though the contests that grew into acceptance over the years throughout the world.

Hoppy was inducted into *International Surfing* magazine's Hall of Fame in 1996.

Lewis "Hoppy" Swarts was the stuff of which the early surf pioneer was made—good citizen surfers who took it upon themselves to organize America's national surfing contests, thereby showing residents of the beach towns along the coasts that surfing was a fun watersport for the whole family. Of course, when the surf was up, it was time to go surfin'! This is Hoppy Swarts in the early 1930s at Hermosa Beach, California. *Doc Ball*

Dick Metz started off as an avid surfer during the 1950s, searching for surf around the world before he went commercial and created a major chain of Hobie Surf and Sport Shops.

Dick Metz
Sport of Kings Conservator

Dick Metz was a surf prognosticator way out in front of the commercial surf train coming down the line. Metz saw it coming early on. After an adventurous solo exploratory surfari "searching for surf" mostly in Africa, and long before *The Endless Summer* troop started its film trip, Metz joined Hobie Alter and then carefully propelled the Hobie Surf and Sports enterprises nationwide. His methodical grassroots-oriented surf retail shop success came in part because of his recognition of the core surfing customer: those surfers who were true aficionados of the sport. Without that insight and surfing experience, Dick most likely would have taken a little longer to become successful.

Once again a surfing visionary, Dick moved on from the retail surf shop business to his nagging personal problem of finding a place to store his 250 antique surfboard collection that he mustered over half a century. The boards needed the light of day and surfing needed a professionally managed, well financed, permanent, for the lack of a better word, "museum." With a little help from his friend, surfer and collector Spencer Croul, and his longtime buddies, Metz opened the Surfing Heritage Foundation in San Clemente, California, a place where surfing can be studied and embraced.

A surfer aficionado with a dream and a vision of preserving the Sport of Kings for future generations, Dick put his money, effort, and organizational skills into making the Surfing Heritage Foundation a reality. "The whole purpose is way more than just to have a building with surfboards on display, although that is part of it," he said.

Dick Metz came from the era when you slept on the beach, made your own boards, and could only take 20-minute go-outs in California's cold waves, which makes him the surfer with the connection to surfing's enchanting past.

"Surfing, the lifestyle, and surf culture all need to be preserved, recorded, and archived."

—*Dick Metz*

Randy Rarick lives the lifestyle that's the envy of all those surfers who love to pile in their wagons stacked with boards and speed off into the night with a dream of finding that secret spot. Randy has searched for surf in more than 60 countries—and is still counting and still looking.

Randy Rarick
At the Vanguard of Professional Surfing

From the beginning, before he got into the business side of surfing, Randy Rarick was in the very "good surfer" class. Randy was born in 1949. Later, under the watchful eye of the legend, Rabbit Kekai, Randy began a lifelong surfing career that's allowed him to surfari around the world searching for surf.

On his home grounds in Hawai'i, Randy's surfing accomplishments in the competitive surfing world were notable. When he was 18 years old, he won the Hawai'ian State Surfing Championship and three years later got into the semi final of the World Contest held in Victoria, Australia.

Randy was good enough to be invited to participate in the classic Duke Kahanamoku Invitational and also surfed in the Smirnoff Pro Am.

When it came to making a living, Randy took up the planer and, with guidance from legendary pioneers George Downing and Dick Brewer, he was able to work for a multitude of surfboard manufacturers, including Surf Line Hawaii, Dewey Weber, and Lightning Bolt.

Randy's claim to international fame came by way of his pioneering of professional surfing through his partnering up with former world champion, Hawai'i's Fred Hemmings. Together they put together the International Professional Surfing (IPS) circuit, which has become the Association of Surfing Professionals (ASP). Randy and Fred also created the Hawaiian Triple Crown mini-series, which in turn became the internationally acclaimed best professional surfing contests.

Randy Rarick's successful multitasking efforts in the name of surfing will be his legacy.

Bob and Bill Meistrell

Body Glove Co-founders

Bob and Bill Meistrell were the twin surfers who bought the Dive N' Surf wetsuit company of Redondo Beach, California, from surfer entrepreneur Bev Morgan. Morgan was the first manufacturer of commercial wetsuits for divers. In 1953, the Meistrells became partners with Morgan and later took over ownership.

The surfer's wetsuit had a slow start. Surfers rejected it at first. They preferred to surf with just surf trunks in the cold winter months. The early suits were uncomfortable, tough to get in and out of, and caused rashes. Dale "The Hawk" Velzy pooh-poohed the wetsuit, claiming the idea would fail but later recanted saying he was wrong!

The wetsuit company eventually worked out the design problems, and wetsuits took off in the 1960s to become a major success and the influential surf product during the twentieth century. Prospective surfers became active surfers because they could now comfortably surf in the cold West Coast waters. The increase in the surfer population was due primarily because of the invention of the wetsuit.

In 1965, the brothers introduced their new label, Body Glove, which set into motion a logo that was appropriate for their tailored-fit styling.

The Meistrells' Body Glove company sponsored the Professional Surfing Association of America and put up $31,725 for the 1989 Trestles event—the richest first-place prize money at the time.

Bob and Bill Meistrell came to surfing and diving like kids who didn't want to grow up—and they did their best not to. Their wetsuit business, which allowed them to enjoy their dreams, contributed the main ingredient that surfing needed for it to be accepted and successful with the general ocean-oriented population. *Bev Morgan*

Cecil Lear

Surf Culture Organizer

Cecil Lear started surfing late in his life at 32, but just in time for the surfing 1960s and to watch it go ballistic. It seemed that everybody got the calling on the East Coast, which fit perfectly with Cecil's organizational skills. The soft-spoken, quiet surfer methodically and carefully put together the pieces of the Eastern Surfing Association, along with New York surfer Rudy Huber in 1967, and launched it in 1968. Cecil has been on the board of directors of the ESA for 40 years and counting.

Kanvas by Katin recognized Cecil for his organizational contributions to surfing by awarding him their Outstanding Surfer Award and Surfer's Cup in 1968.

In 1996, the East Coast Surfing Legends Hall of Fame asked Cecil Lear to join them. He did.

Cecil Lear has served East Coast surfers tirelessly, diligently, and as a father in one way or another ever since 1963 when he first established the New Jersey Surfing Association and then later the Eastern Surfing Association. *Dick Graham*

Dave Shipley has been judging surfing contests for more than twenty years. A "good surfer," Dave will take advantage of any opportunity to catch a few waves before and after events. *Tom Servais*

Jack Shipley
International Master Judge

Jack Shipley caught his first wave as a nine-year-old gremmie on the South Shore of Oahu. So, while growing up in the surfing environment, it seemed natural to get involved with the surf culture. After a stint of due diligence in running some of the local surf shops in Honolulu eventually, Shipley and emerging surf star Gerry Lopez opened the Lightning Bolt Surf Shop in Honolulu. A natural and insightful surf merchant, Jack increased Lightning Bolt's sales and image by getting an international team of superstars to ride Bolt Surfboards, thereby endorsing them. They were very good boards made by the best shapers in the Hawai'ian Islands, and it worked. The Lightning Bolt brand under Jack's tutelage became the popular go-to brand in Hawai'i's surf community with a reputation far beyond its local status. Shortly thereafter, Jack augmented "the strike" into a recognized world brand through an international licensing program.

Jack's personal pursuits followed a different route, and he took on the new path of judging surfing contests in 1966. In 1970, Jack was chosen to be one of the original judges for the first Pipeline Masters, and he has continued to judge the event without missing a contest for 38 years and still counting.

Jack Shipley has devoted close to a half century of his life supporting the Sport of Kings. In both professional and amateur surfing, he has consistently judged and guided surfing through its growing pains.

Jack, right, and Davy Shipley have witnessed more surfers worldwide than anyone else. For a combination of time that has stretched over a half a century, the two have been judging contests at all levels around the world, from Ireland to France to Brazil to Australia, etc., beginning in 1966. *John Bilderback*

Because he was a surfer first, Robert McKnight didn't have to be told what surfers were about or how to make what surfers liked. This insight allowed McKnight to grow his company, run by surfers, and support the sport he loves the way the surfers want to be supported, through specialized surf magazines, surfing trade shows, and international amateur and professional surfing contests. In his way, McKnight has contributed a great deal to the Sport of Kings in a positive and intuitive manner, which is the best anyone can do. *Tom Servais*

Robert McKnight
Surfing CEO

Bob McKnight began surfing when he was 12 years old, and in 1989, he was quoted (out of context) that he was "scared shitless to get a real job." Spoken like a true surfer.

McKnight's "real job" became the CEO of Quiksilver, an international surfwear company, a heavy-duty description job by any standards. Probably because McKnight comes from the world of surfing, the business of running Quiksilver was fun and a nice extension of his surf lifestyle.

The one thing about starting up a surfing business that seems to bear out is that in order to be really successful in the surfing market, it works best to be a surfer and therefore really know your customer. There's a watery graveyard of would-be surf brands that simply did not "get" what surfing and surfers were all about. McKnight understood surfing's nuances, habits, needs, arguments, and devotion to riding waves, because he is a surfer himself. He understood the purity of the hard-core surfers' viewpoints and supported their quest.

Surfing was lucky when it got advocate Bob McKnight, who through the Sport of Kings and Quiksilver, gave surfers a "cool" status and set the bar for other surf companies to follow.

Gordon Merchant
Billabong Visionary

Gordon Merchant began his surfing lifestyle in the late 1950s in a small surf town in Australia called Maroubra, where he was a member of the local surf club. A surfer and shaper in his early days, he was able to sustain his surf lifestyle and his travels with his shaping skills while on the road. During the 1970s, Merchant created a new design concept for surfboard function with a "tucked-under edge" that featured down rail speed with 50-50 rails that combined to make the board faster and more maneuverable. This design is valid to this day.

Surfwear manufacturers seem to get started by selling their products from the trunks of their station wagons. Billabong, the international core surfwear brand, had its humble beginnings that way in 1970, with Mrs. Merchant doing the needlework and Gordon doing the low-key sales approach. Between them they sewed together a core following. The first Billabong board shorts were in need of tweaking, which the Merchants did over the years, as Gordon quickly came into his own as surfing's talented new marketing genius.

By having professional surfers wear the Billabong brand worldwide and by also sponsoring pro contests, coupled with well-placed retail outlets and aligned acquisitions, Gordon took his simple beginnings to a "rags to riches" achievement (pun intended).

First a surfer, then a shaper, Gordon Merchant then became the chairman of the international mega surfwear firm, Billabong Australia. *Tom Servais*

Bev Morgan bucked the tide when he first introduced the surfing wetsuit concept to the public in 1959. It wasn't long before the guiding philosophy of Mickey Muñoz—who said in a Dive and Surf wetsuit advertisement that "it's better to be warm than cold"—took hold. *Bev Morgan family archive*

Bev Morgan
Pioneer Wetsuit Inventor

Bev Morgan started surfing in California in 1946 when he was 13 years old. He was considered by his peers to be a "good surfer" but was better known as the guy who invented the commercial wetsuit, not only for ocean divers, but for surfers, too. The surfers were reluctant at first, however.

"They looked like seals and only sissies would wear one," Morgan said. Undaunted, Morgan pulled together a group of top surfers and gave them each a free wetsuit to test out for him. That event contributed to the phenomenal rise of surfing like no other except for the introduction of light foam boards. Wetsuits opened the door for year-round surfing worldwide, making surfing available for all ages and sexes.

Bev sold his Dive N' Surf shop to the Meistrell Brothers in 1953, and he went on to be an associate editor for John Severson's *Surfer* magazine. As a staff photographer (he developed his own color film), Bev shot three *Surfer* covers and authored several feature articles.

Bev Morgan never asked for and never got the acclaim he deserved for his creativity and foresight regarding surfing. The wetsuit is his legacy.

Jack O'Neill
Wetsuit Vanguard Surfrider

Jack O'Neill was pointed out by *Surfer* magazine as one of the "25 most influential surfers of the 20th century" because of his vanguard pioneering of the surfer's wetsuit.

Jack was born in 1923 and started his surfing lifestyle in the late 1930s. After college, he opened his first surf shop in a simple beachfront garage at Ocean Beach in San Francisco, California. Then in 1959, he moved to nearby Santa Cruz, where his current shop is located.

The O'Neill wetsuit creation started humbly in 1952 with a neoprene vest and steadily grew to be one of the leading wetsuit manufacturers in the world.

Always humble, always low-key, Jack kept a low profile all through his company's remarkable climb.

In 1991, O'Neill was included in the Walk of Fame and the Surf Industry Manufacturers Association (SIMA) gave Jack O'Neill its Waterman's Achievement Award in 2000.

Jack O'Neill began making O'Neill wetsuits in 1952. By the end of the golden 1960s, O'Neill had moved his Santa Cruz company to world-leading status. *Jack O'Neill collection*

Terry "Tubesteak" Tracy
Captain of Malibu Beach

A "good surfer," Terry Tracy loved to disguise his surfing skills with his Hollywood personality. Terry's capability of "clown surfing" proved he had the athletic ability, yet he always said where Dora ruled the wave, he handled the beach.

"Tubesteak"—obviously a nickname that begs curiosity—was the famous Captain of Malibu Beach, and he ran it like an exclusive, members-only surf club, known affectionately as "The Pit" or "The Dump," which was their squatter's space on the beach. Tubesteak defined core surfers by living the surfing lifestyle on the beach in a shack and avoiding work at all costs.

There are many coconut wireless descriptions of how Kathy Kohner got her nickname, Gidget. Tubesteak stakes out that historic claim, as he describes their meeting for the first time:

"'What do you have in that bag?' You know kinda like little red riding hood . . . 'What do you have in that bag?' Kathy says, 'Oh, it's a peanut butter-and-radish sandwich.' Tubesteak: 'I'll tell you what, let us have that sandwich and you can go out with the surfboard.' Kathy says, 'OK.' She gives us the sandwich, so she takes the board and goes into the water. So she comes back in, and she didn't do very well at all. She was, you know, she was a novice. She came back out of the water and says, 'Well, I have some more Fig Newtons up in the car, would you like some of those?' 'Sure.' So she went up and got the Fig Newtons and brought them down. So we had this peanut butter sandwich and the Fig Newtons . . . and she says, 'I have plenty of food at home and you are more than welcome to it.' I said 'OK, Gidget, we'll see you around.'"

Terry "Tubesteak" Tracy's surfing legacy began when he squatted in a self-made shack on the beach at Malibu, California, carefully devoting his time to surfing and consistently avoiding work. Tubesteak set an example of pure surfing priorities for other surfers to follow, an example that will always be a basic part of the surfing adventure. *Leo Hetzel*

PART 11

SURF PHOTOGRAPHERS

THE FIRST PHOTOGRAPHIC RECORD of surfing came through the lenses of late nineteenth-century photographers' cameras.

In Hawai'i the first evidence of surf photography took place on Oahu with the famous Waikiki beach boys as subjects. As time progressed, the cameraman did, too, documenting the revival of this ancient Sport of Kings.

Soon, surf photography spread through the surfing world and grew into a science of long lenses, waterproof cameras, high-speed film, and stop-action photos. Today, professional surf photographers cover the earth going wherever the surfers are, shooting from the beaches, the impact zones, from helicopters and boats.

All of this was for the art of surf photography, for the love of surfing, and for the feeding of these images to the surfing magazines and books that depicted the action and lifestyle of the waveriders, for the world to witness. Today's surf photographers are considered to be the "go-to" source for creative action surf shots. Thanks to these individuals, the surfing story was and continues to be beautifully told. The written word has its place, but the surf photograph captures that fleeting moment in time.

John "Doc" Ball
Pioneer Master Surf Photographer

John Ball was a pioneer of surf photography during the early half of the twentieth century's surfing movement in California.

A prolific surf photographer, "Doc" did it all by simply shooting diligently and consistently the surf community and its surfriders, along the West Coast of America. He documented the awakening of the California surfrider movement. Doc's photographs appeared in *Look*, *Life*, and *Popular Mechanics*, as well as other popular media. In 1946, Doc printed 500 copies of his now famous photo book *The California Surfrider*. Later, the edition sold in the $2,000-plus range to surfing aficionados. Contemporary California surf photographers consider Doc to be the founder of their craft.

Doc Ball was also an ardent surfrider who was instrumental in developing and organizing the famous Palos Verdes Surf Club (PVSC) in 1935. LeRoy Grannis became a member of the PVSC and followed Doc's example by photographing and documenting California's surfing history.

John "Doc" Ball was the perfect embodiment of the dedicated pioneer surf photographer, and he was first to document just about every aspect of the emerging surfing lifestyle during the 1930s. *Tom Blake*

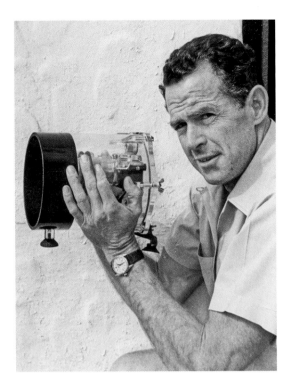

Early on, Dr. Don James was a fan of pioneer photographers John "Doc" Ball and Tom Blake. When his turn came in the 1960s, Don documented the Santa Monica surf area and the San Onofre surf beach near San Clemente before turning to Hawai'i, where he set the standard for tight, well-framed, beautiful color surf photography from the land and the ocean. *Dr. Don James family archive*

Dr. Don James
Master of Surf Photography

Dr. Don James was a master of surf photography whose work spanned six decades of the twentieth century. James, a California surfer from Santa Monica, started surfing in 1935 at the age of 14. Dr. John Ball and Tom Blake were the pioneer surf photographers that must have impressed James, and shortly after starting his surfing career, he began his surf photography journey. Although the water camera was first brought into surfing by Tom Blake, James (who built his own housings) moved water photography to the level of an art form.

James would shoot the North Shore during the winter months, specializing in surf breaks like the Pipeline, Sunset Beach, and Waimea Bay. His shot of John Peck grabbing a rail at the Pipeline is considered a historical classic, as are his pictures of legendary pioneer surfers Buzzy Trent, Peter Cole, and Rick Grigg at maxed-out Waimea Bay. However, James' most famous surf photograph was of California's Rusty Miller at Sunset Beach, shot from the water as Miller dropped down the overhead wave with the pitching curl framing his decent. The photo said it all and became the quintessential surf photograph of the 1960s.

When discussing his surf photography philosophy, James pointed out that although he would take an abundance of surf shots, he would only show his best works, the ones he would choose. That way, he kept his reputation under control.

James has been published and exhibited from prewar days through the turn of the century.

Timothy McCullough
A Treasure of Surf Photography

Tim McCullough came from Avalon, a small island 26 miles off the California coast, to Hawai'i in 1959. Three years later, he got wet at Canoes under the guidance of Hawai'ian legend Rabbit Kekai. From there, Tim moved on to his love of photography and with support of noted island photographer Larry Hata, Tim honed his craft mostly though on-the-job training.

In 1962, when John Severson showed *Going My Wave* at the Kaiser Dome at the Hilton Hawai'ian Village, it provided the next step for Tim to combine his love of surfing with his love of surf photography. The result is the meticulous documentation of the early 1960s pioneering of the North Shore of Oahu, capturing the historical rides of such icons as George Downing, Greg Noll, Mark Martinson, Jackie Eberle, Conrad Canha, Mickey Dora, and Butch Van Artsdalen.

Tim's contribution to surfing's twentieth-century film archives is simply a rich historical treasure.

Tim McCullough went quietly about his business of photographing the pioneer surfers of the 1960s, capturing for surf historians those golden years where innocence still lingered.

LeRoy Grannis was a fixture on the surf beaches of California and Hawai'i, standing with his cap and bazooka lens, patiently waiting for that exact moment to snap and record surfing history. *Leo Hetzel*

LeRoy Grannis
Legendary Surfer and Photographer

LeRoy Grannis started surfing in 1931 when surfing was still in its infancy and well below the national interest level. Grannis, known affectionately as "Grannie," was recognized as one of the outstanding "good surfers" in his day. On doctors orders to take up a hobby, Grannie took up the camera and began a long career in methodically photographing local surfers while unintentionally contributing to the national awareness of the curious new sport of surfing taking place along the California coast and on the beaches of Hawai'i. As most professional surf cameramen see themselves, they are in part the current answer to the historical documentation of the world of surfing and all of its nuances and natural beauty. So it was with Grannie in 1959, when he started his new profession by selling 8x10-inch photos to the surfers on the beach in the South Bay of Los Angeles.

Eventually, Grannie moved on to shoot for the national surf magazines in which he was in some cases a partner. Grannie photographed mainly in California and Hawai'i, documenting the early transition from surfing on heavy redwoods to kook boxes to balsa and foam surfboards. Grannie also shot ads for many of the surf companies of the era. He was particularly instrumental in the introduction and emergence of Hang Ten surfwear, by way of his friendships with the best hot young surfers of the era, who appeared in Grannie's Hang Ten advertising photographs.

On the surf culture side, LeRoy Grannis was a charter member in the United States Surfing Association (USSA) and won his share of trophies, placing in the USSA senior division in the United States Surfing Championships at Huntington Beach.

Always a quiet and soft-spoken gentleman surfrider and photographer whose surf roots spanned more than three-quarters of a century, Grannie was inducted into *International Surfing* magazine's Hall of Fame in 1999 and was given a plaque on the Huntington Beach Surfing Walk of Fame.

Ron Stoner
Chronicler of an Era

Ron Stoner came upon the evolution of surfing at just the right time, setting the standards for composition, rich color, and clarity of image that have been his legacy for more than a half-century.

As a young teenager, Ron Stoner photographed the fresh clean, world of surfing's innocent, carefree days of the 1960s and his body of work set the paradigm for colorful, rich surfing photos. Stoner documented the live, original artform called surfing that was taking place in Mexico, California, and Hawai'i.

Stoner began surfing when he was 14, then entered and began climbing the photographer's ladder through the surf media of the era. First *Surfing Illustrated*, in 1963, *Surf Guide Magazine* in 1964, then Ron settled in with *Surfer* magazine, earning masthead credentials. In 1965, John Severson, the editor of *Surfer*, provided Ron with all the tools he would need to search for surf and shoot it, including cameras, lenses, and money, so off he went, surfer-style, free to photograph the lifestyles of the young 1960's surfriders on the run.

Surfer hooked professional editor Patrick McNulty with cartoonist Rick Griffin, creating a series called, "Surf Adventures of Griffin & Stoner," with McNulty writing the surfari script. It was a showcase for Stoner to show the surf adventures and discoveries of an era that could only be described as innocent and harmless. In 1967–1968, Ron's surfing photos were on the cover of *Surfer* six times in a row, a record not likely to be broken any time soon.

One of Ron Stoner's most memorable photos was shot while on location in Mexico. Later, Ken Auster, a Laguna Beach surf artist, blended acrylic with torn paper, painted Bill Fury (the Clam), on the nose with his surf buddy, Tom Leonardo, paddling out with his arms raised over his head, "touchdown" style, signaling the classic bonding and the connected feeling that surfers share while surfing.

Ron Stoner's documentary photos during the 1960s of young surfriders on surfari, looking for surf, finding it, and riding those waves with nobody else out, were the embodiment of the free-spirited era.

Art Brewer
Timeless Innovator, Master Surf Photographer

Art Brewer has chased vagabond surfers around the world ever since he started as a fledgling surf photographer during the 1960s. By doing so, he has documented the soulful years of surfriding worldwide. *Grant Ellis*

Art Brewer has been dragging cameras, lenses, tripods, and cases around the world since 1968 when he began shooting for *Surfer* magazine. As a teenager from Laguna Beach, Brewer rode his first wave when he was 12 and then slipped into surf photography. Over the years, Art has produced a body of work that is considered to be innovative and timeless by the international and surfing mainstream magazines he shoots for, as well as by his surf photographer contemporaries. Art is one of the few surf photographers who by definition and acclaim, is a master of surf photography.

Warren Bolster

Surf Photography Innovator

In 1970, Warren Bolster pulled off one of those far-out, hard-to-believe stunts. He shot his first roll of color film using a brand-new waterproof camera for the first time—and took a cover shot for *Surfing* magazine! Talk about hitting the jackpot; what's better than that for a beginner at surf photography?

Inspired, Bolster went onto his professional surf photography career working first for *Surfing*, then *Surfer*, and eventually *Skateboarder*, where he held staff photographer titles and associate editor and editor positions.

Over time, Warren gained the reputation of photographing from unusual and creative angles, sometimes from helicopters, or using a water camera mounted on a surfboard. *The Surfer's Journal* featured his creative work in a feature titled "The 50% Solution," where all the photos were shot above and below the ocean's surface.

Before Warren was a surf photographer, he was a surfrider who started surfing in Australia. After moving to Cocoa Beach, Florida, he got into competitive surfing and gained a reputation as a hot contender.

Warren Bolster was brought into the East Coast Surfing Legends Hall of Fame in 2000.

Warren Bolster was an all-around surfer starting out in Australia, then competing with honor out of Coco Beach, Florida, before taking up professional water photography and working as an associate editor for *Surfer*.

Dan Merkel

Impact Zone Photographer

Dan Merkel was considered to be an on-the-job student surf photographer when he first got his surf shots published in 1969, a year after he got his first professional camera. That soon changed when he went to the North Shore of Hawai'i and got to work. His fresh remarkable photos were mostly shot from the impact zone, giving a creative view of surfing that hadn't been seriously exposed until Merkel ventured into the pit. In 1978, Merkel was the photographer who got most of the water shots for John Milius' *Big Wednesday*. Yet, it was felt that Dan's real legacy lies in the work he did on *Free Ride*, the 1970s surf movie that captured the essence of that surfing era.

As a core surfer, Merkel first got wet in 1963, placed fourth in the master's division of the 1972 United States championships, and continued to surf all through his career.

Dan Merkel gained international respect for pioneering the shooting of still photography from within the impact zone.

Jeff Divine's appreciation of the surfing world around him is illustrated not only with his beach and water photography but with casual portraits of the surf culture's icons. *Tom Servais*

Jeff Divine
Master of Surf Photography

Where would surfing be if it wasn't for the surf photographer? Except for the coconut wireless, a lot if not most of what is the recorded essence of surfing would be lost.

Jeff Divine began surfing when he was 14, and he started his photography career in 1965. When he was 18 years old, *Surfer* magazine published Divine's photography and later hired him as a staff photographer. Eventually, he worked up to be the magazine's photo editor. Over more than four decades, Jeff has accumulated a body of work that has earned him the reputation as one of the best surfing photographers of the twentieth century.

The book *Masters of Surf Photography: Jeff Divine* illustrates the point. With pictures taken above and below and in the water, Jeff has captured for aficionados the beautiful, dangerous, and complex Sport of Kings for future generations.

Peter Crawford
Australia's Legendary Surf Photographer

Through the late 1970s and into the 1980s, Peter Crawford earned the reputation of being Australia's finest, if not best, all-around photographer from land as well as from the water. Along his journey, Peter worked for *Surfer* magazine as a masthead photographer, co-founded Australia's *Waves* magazine, and was one of the first surf photographers to explore the surf breaks along the Indonesian Island chains beyond Bali and Eastern Java.

To facilitate his photography, Peter early on engaged in knee boarding and won the Australian National Knee Board Championships three years in a row, from 1976 to 1978.

Peter was bit by a poisonous snake in Bali and died at the age of 48 on Christmas Day 1999. Australia posthumously inducted Peter into its Surfing Hall of Fame in 2001.

Peter Crawford was on the forefront of surf photographers when he began exploring all those exciting far-away surf spots in the Indonesia island chain and beyond.

Bernie Baker
Surfer, Photographer, Journalist, Judge

Bernie Baker is an enthusiastic "good surfer," which is not the first thought one has when you think of him. To most of his peers, he's a one-man band, capable of playing a multitude of surfing roles often at the same time. First, he is a prolific surf journalist who's written 75 features for *Surfer* alone. As one of the magazine's staff photographers, he's had two cover shots published. He's also contributed to a series of respected books on surfing. Keeping busy on the side, Bernie shoots ads for surf clients, covers the Oahu winter surf scene in the water and out, and shoots the surf for the local newspaper. Then, on the professional surfing circuit, Baker directs The Hawaiian Triple Crown of Surfing, a major contest series held annually along Oahu's North Shore and considered to be the crown jewel of professional surfing contests nationally and internationally.

In 1976, Bernie Baker, the multitasker, won the men's division of Hawai'i's State Surfing Championships, countersinking a well deserved legacy he can take pride in.

Bernie Baker has been a long-time proponent of amateur and professional surfing contests. From behind the scenes, Baker has supported the sport, organized it, photographed it, and judged it—and he surfed to victory in the Hawai'i State Surfing Championship in 1976.

Don King
Up Close and Personal Surf Photographer

Don King is the premier prototype water surf photographer. A Hawai'ian island waterman, he played on the Stanford University national water polo championship team in 1980–1981 and held the high school state speed records. Obviously, Don came to photographing the ominous surf of the North Shore uniquely qualified.

Born in Kailua, on the windward side of Oahu, he began surfing in 1969 at 9 years of age. When he was 14, he entered the Pipeline Impact Zone with a waterproof Instamatic and got his photography career off to a courageous—if not a little impractical—start. Still a teenager, Don submitted his surf water shots to *Surfer* and *Surfing* magazine with immediate success. By 1980, he made the masthead of *Surfing* and four years later at 24 years of age, he was the senior staff photographer.

Don King's surf photography was inventive, which is the life's blood of a photographer if he's to be successful. He specialized in shooting from inside the tube looking out with a wide angle lens. Different and creative, Don took his reputation and work to the Chicago Film Festival, where he won the cinematography award. He then went to *Surfer* magazine, where he and Jeff Hornbaker got best cinematography video honors in 1998. There's more, but the honor that nails it is Don's winning of the 1992 Pipeline Body Surfing Contest.

Don King's photography was featured in the *Surfer's Journal* in 1992 with a body of work that displayed 36 pages of seriously tight and close action shots that featured Don's redefinition of where the camera should and could go.

Servais' camera work in the South Pacific went on to win him five *Surfer* covers.

Tom Servais
The Surf Photographers' Surf Photographer

It comes with the camera trade to become known for one particular photograph when you've shot thousands of pictures. It's not fair, but it often happens. Tom Servais, senior staff photographer for *Surfer* magazine, is known for one special shot he took of Florida surfer Cory Lopez deep inside the cavern at Tahiti's awesome Teahupoo. It's one of those surf pictures that immediately causes an emotional identification with the danger that the rider is surrounded by. In sum, it's the kind of image that takes ones breath away.

PART 12

TOW-IN SURFRIDERS

"WHY CLIMB THE MOUNTAIN?"
the climber was asked. "Because it's there!" came the reply. There's not much more to it than that. A simple question, a simple answer, and as you might expect, big-wave surfers, like mountain climbers, are excited by the very sight of big surf waves. They want to get on top of them and ride them for all they are worth. Sounds crazy, and it probably is.

The problem in riding very big waves is that at a certain point in the endeavor, the surfer needs help. He simply can't paddle fast enough to catch them. Enter the tow-in adventure.

By combining a personal water craft (PWC) with the surfer being pulled along behind like a water-skier, the surfrider can reach the speed necessary to be launched into and down waves bigger than a six-story building. There is a growing band of tow-in surfriders searching the oceans for the biggest sea mountains they can find. They are all exceptional watermen, and some have become masters of the tow-in experience. They were the pioneers in the quantum conquering of Jaws and Outside Log Cabins.

Ken Bradshaw
Master Tow-In Surfrider

If ever a surfrider had a calling to ride big waves, make those very big waves, it was the aggressive and determined Ken Bradshaw. The Gulf Coast is not the place that one would think an international big-wave rider and tow-in surfer would hail from. Yet at age 14, Bradshaw left Texas and began to chase his dream by first hop-scotching to California, then to Hawai'i's fabled North Shore. There, he earned his place in the lineup driven by his desire to ride big waves—the bigger the better. Bradshaw was well known for getting in shape and maintaining his physical condition by surfing and exercising constantly, never to a fault.

So, at 45 years of age, after more than three decades of chasing waves 25 feet or higher, and winning his share of titles and trophies, Bradshaw turned his aggressive quest to the next dimension of riding the biggest of waves, this time with the sling-shot, Jet Ski tow-in method. In 1998, he caught and successfully rode the North Shore's "Outside Log Cabins." The final analysis of the wave was measured to be 65 feet from crest to trough. That sea mountain was the biggest wave ridden in the twentieth century and a crowning achievement defining Ken Bradshaw's legacy.

For some surfers, surfing big waves is in their blood. It has to be; why else would they spend their lives looking at the horizon? Here's another day at the office for Ken Bradshaw.

Burton "Buzzy" Kerbox
Vanguard of Tow-In Surfing

Burton Kerbox, known throughout the surfing world as "Buzzy," was the vanguard pioneer partner in the conquest of the sea waves above the 30-foot level. Buzzy, along with Laird Hamilton, Hawai'i's waterman power surfrider, tore down the last bastion of intimidating beliefs that titanic waves of 50 feet could never be ridden. They decided to challenge Jaws by towing each other in by Zodiac onto 15- to 20-foot waves at first, then with Jet Skis they proceeded to graduate upward to mega-sized surf. They conquered Jaws, the sea waves just off Maui's North Shore, by riding surf so enormous that from that day (circa 1994) everything else seemed to have been reduced to a mere shore break.

Buzzy's pre-tow-in lifestyle began in Kailua, Oahu, Hawai'i's east side. When he was 10 years old, he picked up his board, got wet, and began his assault on competitive surfing. In 1978, he won the world cup at Sunset Beach, Oahu. In 1980, he took the top spot in the Sydney, Australia, Surfabout, winning the biggest cash prize in pro surfing to date: $12,000. An original master surfer and pioneer of Maui's Jaws, Buzzy will forever have his place in the origins of surfing's twentieth century.

When asked why he decided to challenge the giant sea surf of Jaws, Burton "Buzzy" Kerbox said, "To ride waves without anyone else around, that's what got the whole thing started for me." *Brian Bielmann*

Dave Kalama
Legendary Big-wave Board Rider

Maui's Dave Kalama comes from a family of watermen. His father, Ilima Kalama, was a pure-blood Hawai'ian surf champion who won the 1962 West Coast Championship, the preeminent mainland contest of the time held at Huntington Beach, California. Dave Kalama started surfing when he was seven at Newport Beach before moving to Maui, where he took up the new sport of sailboarding and went on to be a champion soon after. One thing led to another, and Dave found himself enamored with the potential of attaching foot straps to his surfboard, allowing for flips, flights, and fun.

In 1992, Kalama joined explorers Buzzy Kerbox and Laird Hamilton in challenging Jaws, Maui, the biggest wave capable of being ridden. The addition of foot straps was the key to surviving the incredible surprising bumps down the wave's face. *Surfer* magazine called Kalama's 35-foot wave at Jaws in 1994 the biggest wave ever ridden to date.

Kalama's surfing legacy stretches beyond riding Jaws. Over time, Kalama excelled in tandem surfing, kite surfing, hydrofoil surfing, and both paddling and surfing canoes.

Hawai'ian surfer Dave Kalama is an all-around master surfer.

Dave Kalama is Hawai'i's all-American surfer with multiple skills including sailboarding, longboarding, paddleboarding, canoe surfing, tandem surfing, kite surfing, and hydrofoil riding. And he has been a pioneer in tow-in surfing. Whew! *Brian Bielmann*

Darrick Doerner
Jaws Pioneer

Darrick Doerner is known for keeping a low profile when it involves the surf media, which is exactly the opposite of his attitude toward Hawai'i's winter big-wave and tow-in surf season.

Darrick Doerner is best known as the third man of the threesome that led to the conquering of Jaws, the Mount Everest of Maui's North Shore, where titanic waves come each year. Along with Buzzy Kerbox and Laird Hamilton, Doerner helped construct the assault on the biggest known rideable waves of the era. It was 1992 when the tow-in experimentation began. The obvious question facing Doerner and his cohorts was how to catch and ride waves far too big and fast to paddle into. Plus, the wave itself might kill you, since nothing that big, with the inevitable wipe-out lurking, had ever been experienced before. It was like the proverbial elephant in the room. Towing the surfer much like you would a water-skier became the chosen method of entry by slinging the surfer alongside the speeding and growing wave and toward the Jaws edge, then hastily speeding away to safety. The boards eventually morphed into a shape of a water ski or snowboard-type design, which was the most obvious and practical equipment since the surfers didn't have to lie down and paddle in to catch the wave.

To take on the last bastion of surfing challenges requires a big-wave mentality. Doerner, from the time he first arrived on the North Shore as a teenager, had his eye on riding really big surf. In 1990, he received accolades from *Surfer* magazine's Readers' Poll and also from the Australian *Surfing Life Magazine* poll for his outstanding performances at Waimea Bay. Doerner placed in the Quiksilver in Memory of Eddie Aikau surf contest at Waimea Bay in 1986 and 1996, respectively.

Doerner, 5 feet, 6 inches and weighing a slight 140 pounds, looked even smaller in 1996 when he rode in the tube at Jaws, a wave appraised to be in the range of 35 feet, forever changing the possible dynamics of big-wave surfing.

Darrick Doerner looks upon contest surfing with ambivalence: "It brings out the wrong feelings."

Mike Parsons
The Big Man of Big Waves

Mike Parsons retired from the Association of Surfing Professionals in 1996 after winning the Professional Surfing Association of America Tour in 1991, taking the award from the likes of Taylor Knox and Rob Machado. Mike then went on to bigger things, like the consistent domination of Todos Santos, a 25-foot big wave just south of Tijuana, Mexico.

But Parsons will go down in surfing's annals as the surfer who rode the "Cortes Bank," an open sea wave that popped up to 60 feet, 100 sea miles off San Diego, California. Mike was photographed, documented, and awarded $60,000 cash by Swell XXL. At the time, it was a record cash prize.

In 2002, Mike Parsons started his assault on Jaws, placing second in that year's contest.

Mike Parsons won the biggest cash prize in surfing history at the time—$60,000—for riding a 60-foot wave at Cortez Bank.

In 2002, Garrett McNamara was towed into Tahiti's Teahupoo, a wave so chilling that just looking at it will cause you to squeeze your legs together and take a deep breath. *Brian Bielmann*

Garrett McNamara

Master Tow-In Surfrider

Garrett McNamara is a quiet, humble, and fearless Jaws pioneer from Hawai'i. Always desiring to keep a low profile, McNamara entered into his surfing life when he was 13 on the North Shore of Oahu. After a decade of semi-pro surfing, McNamara discovered tow-in surfing. His skill and accomplishments became evident to the surfing world when he and Brazilian Rodrigo Resende won the first Tow-in World Cup in 2002 at Jaws off the island of Maui.

The next year, Garrett McNamara towed into Tahiti's Teahupoo, a wave so intimidating that like a Brahma bull, it really shouldn't be ridden. Then Garrett put a cap on the year by getting tubed at Jaws during the winter's biggest and longest ride, countersinking McNamara into the legendary tow-in status.

Taylor Knox, it seems, will never be able to get away from his legacy of winning the K2 Big Wave Challenge $50,000 prize, even if he wanted to. As legacies go, the K2 Big Wave Challenge is a nice one. If you can get it.

Taylor Knox

Master Big-wave Surfrider

Taylor Knox's legacy will be his surfing a 52-foot paddle in wave at Todos Santos in Baja California, Mexico, in 1998. Everything else, as they say, is details. Taylor's winner-takes-all-ride got him $50,000 from K2's Big Wave Challenge contest.

With that in mind, Taylor had a string of impressive wins to add to his accomplishments. He won the 1995 Professional Surfing Association of America Tour and the 1996 World Surfing Games Men's Division.

In 1998, Taylor Knox's power surfing style landed him the runner-up spot, second to Kelly Slater in *Surfer* magazine's Readers Award Poll. After the turn of the century in 2001, Taylor was ranked #4 in the world.

Laird Hamilton

Master Waterman

There are several levels of a surfer's reputation. For those on the bottom level, there's the "kook surfer" stage, usually afforded to beginning surfers. Then there's the "okay surfer," which doesn't say much. Of course, there's the "good surfer" level where there is acknowledgement that the surfer in question is more than adequate, better than average, probably close to an A-class surfer. (There are a number of subqualifications to this category.) Finally, there is the acclaimed surfer who is anointed by those who know, the peers who have observed the best of the best over a long period of time, the aficionados of surfing. This stage is the "master class" of the hierarchy of surfing.

Laird Hamilton is in this class by himself. He is a master class surfrider. Few surfers have distinguished themselves above all the rest with so much international acclaim. When Laird began his tow-in assault on Jaws, he did not merely ride it in the hopes of surviving, but he actually toyed with the giant wave before bottom-turning into the tube and coming out in spit. Once Hamilton had set the standard at Jaws for all the world to see, surfing those mega waves became attainable. The challenge was on. That inaugural event of surfing waves above the 35-foot level established the new era of big-wave riding.

It would be redundant to list the accomplishments Laird has achieved. It is best to sum it up by saying they're all true.

An acknowledged twentieth-century "master class" surfrider, Laird Hamilton is the perfect embodiment of the skill and spirit of surfing.

Laird rides Jaws. *Tom Servais*

Index